[LIFE]

LIVING
IN THE
BRACKETS

A SELF HELP BOOK ON

UNFORTUNATELY
HOW WE LIVE

[within the boundaries]

by

ANKI JAIN

DEDICATION

To every individual who never realise that they are, and to those who felt that they are, trapped within the invisible boundaries of their own making, to those who yearn for a life lived beyond limitations, and to those who courageously dare to step outside their comfort zones. This book is a testament to your resilience and a beacon of hope for your journey of self-discovery.

CONTENTS

PREFACE

We all live within brackets, self-imposed limitations that restrict our perspectives, define our choices, and shape our experiences. These brackets, formed by societal expectations, cultural norms, and ingrained beliefs, often hold us captive to a life that feels smaller than the vast potential we carry within.

In this book, we embark on a journey through the lives of ordinary Indians who grapple with these invisible boundaries. We explore the complexities of personal growth, the power of challenging our own beliefs, and the liberation that comes from breaking free from the confines of our comfort zones. Through relatable narratives, insightful observations, and practical exercises, we will delve into the profound impact of our choices, the power of self-awareness, and the transformative journey of finding our true selves.

INTRODUCTION

Imagine a life where your potential is unburdened by self-imposed limitations, where your choices are driven by your own aspirations, and where your experiences are shaped by your own desires. This is the life that lies beyond the brackets we create for ourselves.

This book is an invitation to embark on a journey of liberation. We will explore the commonalities of human experience, the universal need for meaning and connection, and the power of embracing change. We will dissect the often-invisible forces that shape our lives, the societal pressures that mold our perceptions, and the internal dialogues that guide our decisions.

This book is not simply a collection of stories, but a tapestry of insights woven with empathy and wisdom. We will explore the lives of people who have dared to break free from their self-created cages, who have challenged the norms, and who have redefined success on their own terms. Their stories serve as beacons of inspiration, showing us that it is possible to live a life that is authentic, fulfilling, and truly our own.

1

THE CONFINEMENT OF COMFORT ZONE

Understanding the Comfort Zone

The comfort zone, that cozy cocoon we often retreat to, is an intricate web woven from familiarity, routine, and the reassuring feeling of control. It's the safe harbor where we navigate the choppy waters of life with a semblance of predictability. It's the place where we feel comfortable, where we know the rules, and where we can confidently anticipate outcomes.

Imagine a familiar, well-worn path winding through a lush forest. This path, with its familiar curves and bends, represents your comfort zone. It's the path you've traversed countless times, the path you've come to rely on. You know every twist and turn, every fallen log, every rustling leaf. It's safe, predictable, and provides a sense of security.

However, this path, though familiar, might not lead to the breathtaking views, the hidden waterfalls, or the majestic peaks that lie beyond. It might not lead to the vibrant tapestry of experiences and growth that life has to offer. It's the path of the known, not the path of the unknown, and the unknown often holds the key to unlocking a more fulfilling, richer, and more authentic life.

Why does our comfort zone feel so safe? Because it's a space where we avoid the discomforts of the unknown. It's a space where we minimize risk, where we stay within the boundaries of what feels familiar and predictable. It's a space where we avoid the unsettling sting of failure, the gnawing fear of the unknown, and the potential for discomfort.

Think of it like a warm, inviting blanket on a chilly night. It shields us from the elements, provides a sense of warmth and security, and allows us to rest comfortably. We might stay wrapped in this blanket for a long time, finding comfort in its familiarity. But, if we never venture out from beneath its embrace, we might miss the beautiful sunrise, the refreshing breeze, and the exciting possibilities that lie beyond.

The comfort zone can be a double-edged sword. It can be a source of security and stability, providing a foundation from which to explore the world. But it can also become a cage, a self-imposed prison that restricts our growth, limits our experiences, and stifles our potential. It's a paradox: the very space that provides comfort can also become a barrier to our growth and fulfillment.

The comfort zone can manifest in many ways. It can be a job we've held for years, even if it no longer excites us, a relationship that feels comfortable but lacks depth, or a set of beliefs that we've held onto for a lifetime, even if they no longer serve us. It can be the fear of speaking up in a meeting, the anxiety of trying a new recipe, or the hesitation to take on a new challenge.

It's important to acknowledge that there is nothing inherently wrong with seeking comfort and familiarity. It's a natural human instinct to crave safety and security. But it's also crucial to recognize that our comfort zones can become limitations, invisible walls that prevent us from fully embracing life's possibilities.

The comfort zone can be a powerful tool for self-preservation, but it can also be a self-imposed barrier to growth and fulfillment. It's a space we might find ourselves returning to time and again, seeking solace from the uncertainties of the world. However, it's essential to remember that the most meaningful growth, the most transformative experiences, and the greatest sense of purpose often lie beyond the walls of our comfort zones.

As you embark on this journey of self-discovery and growth, consider this: what lies beyond your comfort zone? What awaits you beyond the familiar paths you've always taken? The journey might be challenging, the path might be bumpy, but the rewards are immeasurable.

Embrace the discomfort of stepping outside your comfort zone. Allow yourself to be challenged, to grow, and to discover the boundless possibilities that life has to offer. The journey might be daunting, but the rewards are worth the effort.

The Illusion of Safety

The illusion of safety within the comfort zone is a siren song, luring us into a false sense of security. It whispers promises of peace and stability, urging us to remain within the familiar confines of our known routines, beliefs, and experiences. However, this perceived security comes at a steep price – it hinders our growth, stifles creativity, and limits our potential.

Imagine a lush, vibrant garden, teeming with life and color. This garden represents the boundless possibilities of life, brimming with experiences, knowledge, and opportunities for personal growth. However, within this garden, we erect invisible walls – our comfort zones – that confine us to a tiny patch of ground. This patch, though safe and familiar, pales in comparison to the vastness of the garden beyond. We might be content with the familiar blooms within our little patch, but we miss out on the breathtaking beauty and variety that lies beyond our self-imposed boundaries.

The comfort zone, like a cocoon, offers temporary protection but ultimately restricts our ability to spread our wings and soar. It lulls us into a state of complacency, where we become accustomed to the familiar, shying away from the unknown. But the truth is, staying within the confines of the familiar, while seemingly safe, can become a cage. It can stifle our potential, limit our growth, and prevent us from experiencing the full richness and depth of life.

The illusion of safety within our comfort zones stems from our fear of the unknown. The unfamiliar can be daunting, triggering anxieties and doubts. Stepping outside our comfort zones means embracing uncertainty, vulnerability, and the possibility of failure. This fear, however, often overshadows the potential for growth, learning, and fulfillment that lies beyond our self-imposed limitations.

Take the example of a talented musician who has always played only classical music. Within the comfort zone of their familiar genre, they feel safe and confident. They fear venturing into other musical styles, fearing ridicule or rejection. However, by staying confined to classical music, they deny themselves the chance to explore new sounds, discover their true musical voice, and connect with a wider audience. The fear of venturing into the unknown becomes a barrier to their growth and potential.

This fear of the unknown can manifest in various ways. We might avoid challenging conversations, resist pursuing new passions, or hesitate to take risks that could lead to greater fulfillment. We cling to the safety of our comfort zone, even if it means staying stagnant and unfulfilled.

It's important to acknowledge that comfort zones can be a double-edged sword. While they provide a sense of security and stability, they can also become a trap that prevents us from reaching our full potential. The key is to recognize when our comfort zone becomes a barrier to growth and to find the courage to step outside of it.

Stepping outside our comfort zone is not a call to abandon our existing habits or routines entirely. Instead, it's about finding the courage to take small, intentional steps towards the unknown, gradually expanding our comfort zone with each new experience.

Here are some ways to recognize the illusion of safety within our comfort zones and start taking steps towards a more fulfilling life:

Identify Your Limiting Beliefs: Our beliefs about ourselves, the world, and our capabilities can create invisible walls that confine to us within our comfort zones. Take a moment to reflect on your beliefs about your abilities, your limitations, and your potential. Are these beliefs serving you, or are they holding you back?

Challenge Your Fears: The fear of the unknown is a powerful force, but it can be overcome. Recognize that the fear of failure or rejection often outweighs the potential for growth and reward. Take small, manageable steps to confront your fears. The more you do, the less intimidating the unknown will seem.

Embrace Failure as a Learning Opportunity: Failure is not the end, but rather a steppingstone on the path to growth. Every failure offers valuable lessons and insights that can help us move forward. Approach mistakes with a willingness to learn and adapt.

Celebrate Your Growth: Stepping outside your comfort zone can be challenging, so it's important to acknowledge and celebrate your accomplishments. Recognize your courage and commitment to personal growth. The more you celebrate your wins, the more motivated you will be to continue pushing your boundaries.

Remember, stepping outside your comfort zone is not about achieving perfection or becoming someone you're not. It's about recognizing your potential, embracing the unknown, and living a life that's true to yourself. The journey may not always be easy, but it's through stepping outside our comfort zones that we discover our true selves and unlock the incredible possibilities that life has to offer.

<u>Recognizing Personal Boundaries</u>

Imagine a cozy, familiar room, a haven from the world outside. The walls are adorned with memories, the air thick with the scent of comfort. This is your comfort zone, a safe space where you feel understood, accepted, and secure. It's where you retreat after a long day, seeking solace and familiarity.

But what if this haven, this safe space, is also a cage? What if the walls that offer comfort also confine and restrict your growth? This is the paradox of the comfort zone. While it offers security, it also limits our potential, keeping us trapped in a familiar, predictable routine.

We all have comfort zones, invisible boundaries we build around ourselves, shaping our perceptions and dictating our choices. These boundaries, often self-imposed, stem from a combination of factors: past experiences, learned behaviors, societal expectations, and even fear. We develop a sense of security within these boundaries, a familiar framework that defines our identity and provides a sense of belonging.

Yet, within the safety of our comfort zones, we often miss out on opportunities for personal growth, new experiences, and meaningful connections. It's like a well-worn path in the forest, familiar and safe, but ultimately leading nowhere new. The fear of the unknown, of venturing outside the comfort zone, can be a powerful deterrent.

The illusion of safety within the comfort zone can be a deceptive trap. While it provides a temporary sense of security, it ultimately hinders our progress and prevents us from exploring our full potential. Imagine a talented artist who never ventures beyond their preferred style, a gifted musician who always plays the same chords, or a writer who only writes about familiar themes. Their skills remain stagnant, their potential untapped, all because of the fear of stepping outside their comfort zones.

It's crucial to recognize these self-imposed limitations, to identify the invisible boundaries that define our comfort zones. It's a journey of self-discovery, of confronting our fears, and questioning our assumptions.

To understand the extent of these limitations, let's explore some real-life stories. Take, for instance, the case of a young woman named **Anjali**, who had always dreamt of being a doctor. Yet, the pressures of societal expectations and the fear of failure held her back. She ended up pursuing a safe, predictable career path, one that aligned with her family's expectations but not with her true aspirations.

There's also the story of **Amit**, a young man who felt compelled to live up to his father's expectations of becoming an engineer. He excelled in his studies, secured a prestigious job, and lived a life that outwardly appeared successful. However, his heart wasn't in it. He dreamt of being a writer, of crafting stories that would touch people's lives. But fear held him back, preventing him from pursuing his true passion.

These stories, although fictional, reflect the reality of countless individuals who are trapped within the confines of their comfort zones. The weight of societal expectations, fear of judgment, and the desire for acceptance often lead us to make choices that are not aligned with our true selves.

The journey of breaking free from the confines of the comfort zone is not about abandoning security or embracing recklessness. It's about challenging our own perceptions, embracing calculated risks, and finding the courage to step outside the familiar.

So how do we start this journey? How do we recognize the limitations of our comfort zones and begin to challenge them? The first step is to become self-aware. To introspect and examine our choices, our beliefs, and the factors that influence our decisions.

Ask yourself these questions:

- What activities do I avoid because they feel uncomfortable or challenging?
- What fears or insecurities are holding me back from pursuing my passions?
- What are the consequences of staying within my comfort zone, both personally and professionally?

By honestly reflecting on these questions, you can gain valuable insights into the limitations you've created for yourself. Once you've identified the barriers, it's time to start taking small, intentional steps to push your boundaries.

Start with something manageable, something that doesn't require a massive leap of faith. Maybe it's trying a new recipe, attending a social gathering outside your usual circle, or taking a short course in a subject you've always wanted to learn. Every step outside the comfort zone, no matter how small, builds confidence and reinforces the belief that you can handle the unknown.

Remember, change is a process, not an event. There will be moments of doubt, discomfort, and even setbacks. But each hurdle you overcome will contribute to your growth, building resilience and a deeper understanding of your capabilities.

The stories of Anjali and Amit serve as reminders that the comfort zone is not a permanent destination. It's a temporary shelter, a steppingstone on the journey of self-discovery and growth.

As we explore the deeper significance of the comfort zone and the potential for growth beyond it, we'll delve into the stories of individuals who've embraced change, defied expectations, and found true fulfillment in stepping outside their familiar boundaries. These stories offer a beacon of hope, demonstrating that the journey beyond the comfort zone is not only possible but also transformative.

<u>Stories of Silent Struggles</u>

The comfort zone, that seemingly safe haven we all seek, can often become a cage, limiting our growth and potential. It's a place of familiar routines, predictable outcomes, and the absence of discomfort. While the comfort zone provides a sense of security and stability, it can also trap us in a cycle of stagnation, preventing us from experiencing the full breadth of life's possibilities.

Consider the story of **Priya**, a talented artist who spent years working a corporate job she loathed. She had a steady paycheck, a comfortable routine, and the approval of her family, yet her soul yearned for something more. Priya had a deep passion for painting, but the fear of failing, of not being able to support herself, kept her trapped in a life that was devoid of joy. Every day felt like a monotonous routine, a constant reminder of the creative fire that was slowly dying within her.

Then there's **Amar**, a middle-aged man who spent years in a loveless marriage. He was afraid of the unknown, of facing the loneliness and potential rejection that came with leaving his wife. He had built a life, a family, and a social circle, and the thought of disrupting this carefully constructed world filled him with anxiety. He resigned himself to a life of quiet misery, convinced that staying was the only option, even though it meant sacrificing his own happiness.

These stories are just glimpses into the silent struggles of individuals confined by the invisible walls of their comfort zones. The fear of the unknown, the pressure of societal expectations, and the desire to maintain a sense of control often keep us anchored in familiar territory, even when it no longer serves us. It's a cycle of self-imposed limitations, where the fear of venturing out outweighs the desire for personal growth and fulfillment.

The truth is, comfort zones are often illusions. The sense of safety they provide is a mirage, a deceptive illusion that hides the potential for true growth and happiness. Staying within the confines of our comfort zones may protect us from immediate discomfort, but it also prevents us from discovering the vast potential that lies within us. It's a cycle of self-sabotage, where the desire for stability trumps the yearning for a life that is truly meaningful and fulfilling.

We may convince ourselves that staying within our comfort zones is the safe and responsible choice, but what if that perceived safety is just a fear-based illusion? What if the true risk lies in remaining stagnant, in allowing our dreams to fade into the background noise of our everyday lives? The real risk is not in stepping out of our comfort zones, but in never venturing beyond them.

Recognizing these self-imposed limitations is the first step towards breaking free. It's about identifying the invisible boundaries we've erected around ourselves, the fears and beliefs that keep us tethered to the familiar. It's about acknowledging that the world is a vast and vibrant place, full of possibilities waiting to be explored, but only if we dare to venture beyond the limitations, we've placed upon ourselves.

Think of it like this: imagine a seed trapped in a small pot. It has access to water, sunlight, and nutrients, but its growth is limited by the size of its container. It may feel safe and comfortable in its tiny world, but it's never going to reach its full potential. It needs to be replanted in a larger pot, to be given the space to spread its roots, to grow into a strong, healthy plant.

The same holds true for us. Our comfort zones, like that small pot, may provide a sense of stability, but they ultimately limit our growth. We need to be willing to step out of our familiar containers, to break free from the invisible barriers that confine our potential. We need to embrace the discomfort of change, to face our fears and push beyond our self-imposed limitations. Only then can we truly flourish and live a life that is rich, fulfilling, and aligned with our authentic selves.

The stories of Priya and Amar are not unique. They are reflections of the human condition, of the struggle to break free from the confines of our comfort zones and embracing the unknown. Their stories, and countless others like them, serve as reminders that the path to true fulfillment lies not in the safety of the familiar, but in the courage to step outside and explore the boundless possibilities that life has to offer.

The first step towards this transformation lies in recognizing our own comfort zones, in acknowledging the boundaries we've built around ourselves. It's about understanding the reasons behind our reluctance to change, to embrace the discomfort that comes with stepping into the unknown. It's about questioning our beliefs, our fears, and our self-limiting narratives. It's about challenging the status quo and daring to imagine a life beyond the confines of our comfort zones.

This is not a journey for the faint of heart. It requires courage, vulnerability, and a willingness to embrace discomfort. But the rewards are immense. By stepping outside our self-imposed limitations, we open ourselves up to a world of possibilities, a world where we can truly thrive and live a life that is aligned with our authentic selves.

First Steps to Change

The first step towards breaking free from the confines of your comfort zone is the most daunting, yet the most crucial. It's like taking a deep breath before diving into a pool, the moment of hesitation before the plunge. The fear of the unknown lurks within, whispering doubts and reminding you of the familiar safety of your comfort zone. But it's in this moment of hesitation that the true test of your desire for change lies.

Imagine a young woman named **Radha**, trapped in a comfortable yet unfulfilling corporate job. She spent her days staring at spreadsheets, a constant hum of routine filling her days. Radha had always dreamt of becoming a writer, her heart yearning for the freedom of expression and the thrill of weaving stories. But the fear of failure, the societal pressure of a "stable" career, kept her tethered to her comfort zone. Her comfort zone, however, was a cage of her own making, holding her back from pursuing her passions.

One day, Radha stumbled upon a blog post about "the comfort zone trap." It talked about how staying within one's comfort zone, while seemingly safe, could be a prison for one's potential. Radha was startled. Could her desire for something more be stifled by her fear of the unknown? This was a turning point. Radha recognized the limiting nature of her self-imposed comfort zone, the fear that had held her back for so long. She decided to take the first step, a seemingly small step, but one that held immense significance. She signed up for a creative writing workshop.

Radha's first steps to change were small, deliberate actions that challenged her comfort zone. She began by attending the writing workshop, exposing herself to new ideas and perspectives. Each session was a step outside her comfort zone, each writing exercise a battle against the fear of judgment. Radha found that the fear was not as crippling as she had imagined. Instead, it was a motivator, pushing her to explore her creativity and unleash her hidden potential.

You too can take those first steps. They don't need to be giant leaps, but rather small, consistent actions that nudge you outside of your comfort zone.

Here are some first steps you can take:

1. **Identify your comfort zone:** The first step to stepping out is to acknowledge where you are. Think about your daily routine, your interests, and your interactions. What activities bring you comfort, and what activities do you avoid? This self-awareness is crucial.

2. **Challenge a small habit:** Start small. Instead of trying to overhaul your entire life, focus on one small habit you can change. It could be as simple as trying a new recipe, taking a different route to work, or striking up a conversation with a stranger.

3. **Embrace a new experience:** Step outside your comfort zone by trying something new. It could be a new hobby, a new type of exercise, or even a visit to a new part of your city. The key is to expose yourself to something unfamiliar and challenge yourself to adapt.

4. **Find a support system:** Having a support system is crucial for stepping outside your comfort zone. Talk to friends, family, or a therapist about your goals and fears. Sharing your journey can provide encouragement and accountability, especially during difficult moments.

5. **Celebrate your wins:** Every step outside your comfort zone, no matter how small, is a victory. Acknowledge your achievements and

celebrate your progress. This positive reinforcement will fuel your motivation to keep moving forward.

Remember, change is a journey, not a destination. It's a series of small steps, each one a testament to your courage and your willingness to break free from the constraints of your comfort zone. Radha, with her newfound determination, continued to push her boundaries. She began writing regularly, joining online writing communities, and submitting her work to literary magazines. The initial fear gradually gave way to a sense of empowerment, and Radha discovered a newfound confidence in herself. She learned that her comfort zone, while safe, was not the only way to live.

The journey of stepping outside your comfort zone is not without its challenges. There will be moments of doubt, of fear, and of uncertainty. But it is in these moments that your true strength lies. When you overcome these challenges, you gain a new sense of self-assurance, a newfound appreciation for your own resilience, and a realization that you are capable of far more than you ever thought possible.

Remember, every journey begins with a single step. Take that first step, even if it feels small. Embrace the uncertainty, the fear, and the discomfort. For it is in the realm of the unknown that you will find your true potential.

2

THE WEIGHT OF EXPECTATIONS

<u>Inherited Expectations</u>

The air hung heavy with unspoken expectations, a tangible weight pressing down on the shoulders of every young Indian. From the moment we were born, we were enveloped in a cocoon of societal and familial norms, woven into the very fabric of our existence. These expectations were as familiar as the scent of chai brewing in the mornings, as comforting as the warmth of our grandmother's embrace. But sometimes, this comforting familiarity felt like a cage, limiting our aspirations and stifling our dreams.

Our parents, grandparents, our aunts and uncles, and even our neighbors, all had their own ideas about what we should be, what we should achieve, and how we should live our lives. The pressure to conform to these expectations was often subtle, yet powerful. It whispered in the back of our minds, shaping our choices, influencing our decisions, and casting a long shadow over our futures.

"You should become a doctor," my father would say, his voice laced with the pride of a father who dreamed of his son walking in his footsteps. "It's a respected profession, and you'll be able to take care of yourself."

"Become an engineer," my mother would add, her eyes filled with the hopes of a woman who wanted her daughter to be financially independent. "It's a secure career, and you'll have a good life."

These were not malicious pronouncements, but rather expressions of love and concern, deeply rooted in the traditions and values they had inherited. They believed they were guiding us towards a life of stability and prosperity, a life free from the struggles they had faced. But within those expectations, there was a hidden cost, a price for conforming to a script that had been written for us long before we were born.

This invisible pressure permeated every aspect of our lives, shaping our choices from the moment we woke up to the moment we went to bed. It influenced our education, our career choices, our relationships, and even our hobbies. We were taught to value conformity over individuality, to prioritize family and tradition over personal pursuits.

The pressure to conform was especially intense for young women. From the moment they were born, they were expected to uphold certain standards of behavior and conduct. They were taught to be demure, submissive, and focused on family and domestic responsibilities. These societal expectations were deeply ingrained in our culture, passed down through generations, shaping the narratives we told ourselves about who we were and what our roles in society should be.

"You should be a good wife," my grandmother would often remind me, her voice a gentle yet unwavering reminder of the path she believed I should follow. "Find a good husband, raise a family, and make your parents proud."

These words, spoken with love and good intentions, carried the weight of centuries of tradition, a legacy of expectations that seemed impossible to escape.

Yet, within the heart of every young Indian, there was a silent rebellion brewing. We yearned for a life that was our own, a life where we could define our own paths, pursue our own dreams, and forge our own destinies. We longed to break free from the shackles of expectations to step outside the boundaries that had been set for us, and to embrace the unknown.

The weight of expectations was heavy, but it was not insurmountable. Within us, a spark of defiance flickered, fueled by a deep-seated desire to create a life that was true to ourselves. This was a journey of self-discovery, a struggle to find our own voice amidst the chorus of expectations, a quest to break free from the invisible brackets that confined us.

The path ahead was fraught with challenges, filled with moments of doubt, fear, and self-questioning. But we were not alone. Around us, countless individuals were embarking on similar journeys, challenging the status quo, and pushing the boundaries of what was considered acceptable. They were our inspiration, our reminders that change was possible, that we could rewrite our own stories, and create a life that was truly our own.

It was not a simple path, but a necessary one. The weight of expectations might have been heavy, but it was also a reminder of the love and care that had shaped our lives. We needed to acknowledge the source of those expectations, to understand the motivations behind them, but ultimately, we needed to find the courage to step out of the shadows they cast and embrace the journey of self-discovery.

The journey of breaking free from expectations was not just about defying societal norms or rebelling against family traditions. It was about finding our own identity, defining our own values, and building a life that was aligned with our own aspirations. It was about embracing the power of choice, the freedom to choose our own paths, and the courage to live a life that was true to ourselves.

As I reflect on my own journey, I am grateful for the love and guidance of those who came before me, even if their expectations sometimes felt constricted. Their values instilled in me a strong foundation, a sense of purpose and direction, and a belief in the power of hard work and dedication. But I also recognize that true fulfillment lies in embracing my individuality, in exploring my passions, and in pursuing a life that resonates with my own values.

The journey of breaking free from expectations is not about denying our heritage, but about enriching it. It is about taking the best of what we have been given and adding our own unique voice to the chorus. It is about creating a new narrative, a story of self-discovery, of embracing the unknown, and of living a life that is truly our own.

The path may be challenging, but it is a path worth taking, a journey that leads us towards a life of authenticity, self-acceptance, and fulfillment. The weight of expectations may be heavy, but it is also a catalyst for growth, a reminder that we have the power to rewrite our stories and create a life that is truly our own.

As we step outside the confines of those invisible brackets, we discover the boundless possibilities that await us. We find ourselves not only breaking free from expectations, but also embracing the freedom to define our own destinies, to create a life that is authentic, fulfilling, and true to our own unique spirit. And in that journey of self-discovery, we not only find ourselves, but also unlock the potential within us to live a life that is truly our own.

The Pressure of Conformity

In India, expectations are woven into the very fabric of our lives. From the moment we are born, we are surrounded by a symphony of voices – family, friends, society – all contributing to a chorus of expectations that shape our aspirations and define our paths. These expectations, though often well-intentioned, can be a double-edged sword. While they offer a sense of direction and belonging, they can also impose stifling pressure to conform, inhibiting personal growth and hindering the pursuit of a fulfilling life.

The pressure to conform often stems from the deeply ingrained cultural norms that dictate how individuals should live, behave, and achieve success. These norms can be powerful, dictating everything from career choices to marriage prospects to societal roles. While they provide a sense of order and stability, they can also create rigid boundaries, restricting individuals from exploring their true potential and embracing their unique identities.

Take, for example, the traditional expectations placed upon young women in many Indian families. They are often expected to prioritize marriage and family over personal ambitions, facing societal pressure to conform to the role of a dutiful wife and mother. This pressure can make it difficult for them to pursue their dreams, whether it be a career in a male-dominated field or simply the freedom to choose their own life partners.

Similarly, young men in India are often expected to pursue certain professions, like engineering or medicine, that are deemed respectable and financially secure. They may feel pressure to live up to the expectations of their families and community, leaving little room for exploring passions outside these prescribed paths.

This pressure to conform can have a profound impact on our self-esteem and sense of belonging. We may feel like we are constantly being judged and evaluated, leading to a constant striving for approval and acceptance. This can create a cycle of self-doubt and fear, preventing us from taking risks, pursuing our dreams, and embracing our true selves.

The societal expectations that we inherit can sometimes feel like an invisible weight on our shoulders, a constant reminder of what is expected of us. This can lead to a sense of being trapped, living a life dictated by external pressures rather than our own aspirations.

But the beauty of life lies in its diversity. The pressure to conform can be countered by embracing the individuality that makes each of us unique. The journey of self-discovery is about breaking free from the confines of these expectations and recognizing that our worth is not defined by external validation but by our own internal compass. It's about finding the courage to redefine success on our own terms, to live a life that resonates with our values, and to embrace the power of our own unique narratives.

The stories of individuals who have defied expectations, who have dared to break the mold and forge their own paths, are a testament to the transformative power of self-belief. These stories serve as beacons of hope and inspiration, showing us that it is possible to live beyond the pressure of conformity and create a life that is both meaningful and fulfilling.

Take, for example, the story of a young woman from a traditional family who defied the expectations placed upon her to pursue a career in science. Despite facing resistance from her family, she persevered, determined to make her mark in a field that was traditionally considered "unfeminine."

She went on to become a renowned scientist, not only achieving personal success but also inspiring countless other young women to break free from societal constraints.

Or consider the story of a young man who, instead of following the traditional path of pursuing a career in engineering or medicine, decided to follow his passion for art. He faced skepticism from his family and friends, who questioned his career choice and its potential for financial stability. However, he remained steadfast in his pursuit, ultimately becoming a successful artist, proving that following one's passion can lead to a fulfilling and meaningful life.

These stories highlight the importance of embracing our individuality and the power of defying societal expectations. They remind us that we are not defined by the roles that society assigns us, but by the choices we make and the paths we carve for ourselves.

The journey to break free from the pressure of conformity is not always easy. It requires courage, resilience, and a strong sense of self-belief. It requires a willingness to challenge our own beliefs, to embrace the unknown, and to redefine success on our own terms.

But the rewards are immeasurable. By breaking free from the confines of societal expectations, we gain the freedom to explore our potential, to live authentically, and to create a life that truly resonates with who we are. We discover the power within ourselves to shape our own destinies and to live a life that is both fulfilling and meaningful.

It's important to recognize that breaking free from expectations doesn't mean rejecting the wisdom of our ancestors or the traditions that have shaped our culture. It's about finding a balance between honoring our heritage and embracing our individuality. It's about choosing to live a life that is true to our values, our passions, and our unique potential.

Ultimately, the pressure of conformity can be a powerful motivator for personal growth and transformation. By recognizing the expectations that are placed upon us, by understanding their origins, and by choosing to challenge those expectations, we embark on a journey of self-discovery that leads to a life of greater freedom, authenticity, and fulfillment. It is a journey that begins with a single step, a decision to break free from the confines of our self-imposed limitations and to embrace the boundless possibilities that life offers.

<u>Breaking the Mold</u>

The weight of expectations can be a heavy burden to carry. It's a force that shapes our dreams, our choices, and ultimately, the lives we lead. In India, this force is particularly strong, woven into the fabric of society, passed down through generations like an heirloom. From the moment we are born, we are molded by a web of expectations, a symphony of voices dictating what we should become, how we should behave, and what success should look like.

These expectations can be both nurturing and stifling, offering guidance while simultaneously limiting our potential. They can stem from family, friends, society, and even us. From parents who dream of their children becoming doctors or engineers, to communities that value conformity over individuality, the pressure to meet these expectations can be immense.

Often, these expectations are rooted in good intentions, fueled by love, tradition, and a desire for our well-being. However, when these expectations become rigid, uncompromising, and overshadow our own aspirations, they can morph into a force that hinders our growth and inhibits our happiness.

We see this reflected in countless stories, each a testament to the struggle of living within the confines of these expectations. Take, for instance, the story of **Jiya**, a young woman raised in a traditional family in a small town. Jiya, despite her passion for art, was expected to pursue a career in medicine, a profession that promised stability and social recognition.

Jiya's parents, like many others, saw medicine as a path to a secure future, a safeguard against the uncertainties of life. They believed that pursuing art would be a risky, impractical choice, leading to a precarious life of uncertainty. Their love for Jiya was undeniable, yet their expectations were rooted in a deep-seated fear of her future, a fear they projected onto her.

Jiya, trapped between her own desires and the expectations of her loved ones, found herself torn. She felt the weight of her family's hopes pressing down on her, the whispers of societal approval and disapproval echoing in her ears. For years, she tried to suppress her artistic yearnings, pursuing a medical degree to satisfy her family.

Yet, her artistic spirit refused to be silenced. It flickered in her spare moments, finding expression in stolen hours spent sketching and painting. The act of creation brought her solace, a sense of fulfillment that her medical studies could not offer.

As Jiya delved deeper into her medical studies, the dissonance between her heart and her actions grew stronger. The pressure to conform, to live up to the expectations placed upon her, began to take its toll. She felt a growing sense of dissatisfaction, a void that no amount of academic achievement could fill.

Eventually, Jiya realized that living a life of compromise was not a life worth living. She understood that her happiness lay not in fulfilling her family's expectations, but in following her own path, however unconventional it might seem.

This realization led Jiya to a difficult but necessary decision: to break free from the mold, to defy expectations and pursue her passion for art.

Her decision was met with resistance. Her family, having invested years in her medical education, struggled to understand her choice. Their fears, though rooted in love, were a barrier to Jiya's pursuit of her dreams.

Jiya, however, stood firm. She had tasted the sweetness of her own creative expression, the freedom of pursuing a path that resonated with her soul. She was determined to carve her own destiny, to break free from the shackles of expectations and embrace her true self.

Jiya's journey was not without its challenges. She faced financial hardships, questioning looks from family and friends, and the constant fear of societal disapproval. Yet, she persevered, fueled by her unwavering passion and a deep-seated belief in herself.

Over time, she found a community of artists who supported her, who understood her struggle and celebrated her talent. She honed her skills, her art evolving into a powerful expression of her emotions, her thoughts, and her unique perspective on the world.

Jiya's story is a testament to the transformative power of breaking free from expectations. It highlights the courage it takes to challenge societal norms and embrace our own individuality. Her journey reminds us that true success lies not in fulfilling predetermined roles but in discovering and embracing our own unique passions and aspirations.

But Jiya's story is not unique. Countless others have walked a similar path, defying expectations, embracing their own paths, and finding fulfillment beyond the boundaries of societal norms.

There's **Rahul**, the young man who dared to leave his lucrative engineering career to pursue a passion for dance. His parents, like Priya's, envisioned a future for him filled with stability and financial security. Dance, in their eyes, was an impractical pursuit, a frivolous endeavor.

Rahul's journey was a testament to the power of defying expectations. He persevered, his passion driving him through every obstacle, every moment of doubt. He fought against societal pressure to choose a 'practical' path, proving that a life lived authentically could be just as fulfilling, if not more, than a life lived according to predetermined expectations.

And then there's **Seema**, a young woman from a traditional family who challenged gender roles by becoming a successful entrepreneur. Seema, like Priya, was expected to prioritize marriage and family, to embrace the role of a homemaker. However, she had a vision, a burning desire to build something of her own, to carve her own path in the world.

Seema's journey was filled with hurdles, societal expectations weighing down on her, her family's anxieties echoing in her ears. Yet, she refused to let their concerns deter her. She channeled their doubts into fuel for her ambition, her determination burning brighter with each challenge she faced.

Seema's success was not just about financial gain, but about breaking free from the constraints of traditional gender roles. Her story inspired countless other women, proving that women could pursue their dreams, achieve success on their own terms, and become powerful agents of change.

Each of these stories, Jiya's, Rahul's, and Seema's, are a testament to the transformative power of breaking free from the weight of expectations. They remind us that true fulfillment lies not in conforming to external pressures, but in embracing our own unique paths, pursuing our passions, and living a life that aligns with our true selves.

These stories, and countless others like them, serve as beacons of hope, inspiring us to challenge the societal norms that limit our potential and to embrace the courage to live a life that is authentically ours.

It is in these acts of defiance, in these moments of breaking free from the shackles of expectations, that we discover the true meaning of freedom, the joy of self-expression, and the power of living a life that is truly our own.

<u>Redefining Success</u>

The pressure to conform is a heavy weight, a relentless force that whispers doubts and anxieties into our ears, urging us to abandon our dreams and ambitions in favor of a predetermined path. It tells us that success is measured in external validation, with the approval of others, in the accumulation of material possessions, and in adherence to societal norms. It whispers that happiness lies in achieving the predefined benchmarks, in reaching the destinations society has marked out for us.

But what if success is not a destination, but a journey? What if it is not a ladder we climb to reach the top, but a tapestry we weave with the threads of our own experiences, passions, and aspirations? What if the true measure of success lies not in external achievements, but in the internal satisfaction of living a life aligned with our values, our beliefs, and our authentic selves?

In a world obsessed with quantifiable achievements, it's easy to get caught up in the pursuit of accolades, titles, and material wealth. We chase external validation, seeking approval from society, family, and friends. We strive to fit into predefined molds, to tick off the boxes on the societal checklist of success. But in this relentless chase, we often lose sight of our own inner compass, the unique voice that whispers our true desires and dreams.

Take, for example, the story of **Monali**, a young woman who grew up in a family that valued academic excellence and professional success above all else. She excelled in her studies, earning a prestigious degree in engineering. She landed a high-paying job at a multinational corporation, fulfilling the expectations of her family and society. Yet, deep within her,

Monali felt a gnawing emptiness. Her heart longed for something more, something beyond the confines of her corporate cubicle and the pursuit of material success.

Monali's story is not an isolated one. Countless individuals in India, and indeed across the world, live lives that are dictated by societal norms and expectations. We strive to meet the benchmarks that have been set for us, often sacrificing our own dreams and aspirations in the process.

But what if we dared to redefine success on our own terms? What if we embraced the freedom to chart our own course, to define our own path to fulfillment?

To break free from the weight of expectations, we must first understand the origins of these pressures. Many of these expectations stem from the cultural norms and societal values that shape our lives. In India, for example, traditional values often emphasize family, marriage, and the pursuit of a stable career. These values are ingrained in us from a young age, shaping our perspectives and influencing our choices.

The pressure to conform can come from various sources: family, friends, colleagues, and even us. Parents, for instance, often project their own aspirations and unfulfilled dreams onto their children. They may push them towards specific careers or educational paths, believing it to be the right course for their future. This pressure can be well-intentioned, stemming from a deep love and concern for their children's well-being. However, it can also create a sense of obligation and conformity, limiting their children's exploration of their own passions and interests.

The weight of societal expectations can also be a powerful force, dictating what we believe is acceptable, desirable, and successful. We are bombarded with messages about how to live our lives, what careers to pursue, what relationships to form, and what constitutes success. These messages can be insidious, subtly shaping our perceptions and influencing our decisions without our conscious awareness.

The fear of judgment and rejection can be a powerful motivator for conformity. We fear the disapproval of our peers, the disappointment of our families, and the judgment of society. This fear can lead us to suppress our true selves, to conform to expectations, and to live lives that do not align with our authentic desires.

Breaking free from the weight of expectations is not about defying societal norms or abandoning family values. It is about finding a balance, a harmony between what society expects of us and what our hearts truly desire. It is about recognizing that success is not a one-size-fits-all concept but a deeply personal journey, unique to each individual.

Redefining success is about claiming ownership of our lives, about reclaiming our power to define what matters most. It is about embracing our passions, pursuing our interests, and forging a path that resonates with our souls.

This journey of redefining success is not a linear path, but a winding road filled with unexpected twists and turns. It is a journey of self-discovery, of challenging our limiting beliefs, and of embracing the freedom to be our authentic selves. It requires courage, resilience, and a willingness to step outside our comfort zones.

As we embark on this journey, it's crucial to remember that we are not alone. There are countless others who have navigated similar paths, who have challenged expectations and redefined success on their own terms. We can draw inspiration from their stories, their struggles, and their triumphs.

Stories of Breaking the Mold

The weight of expectations can be particularly challenging in India, a country rich in cultural diversity and tradition. But within this rich tapestry of traditions, there are countless stories of individuals who have dared to break the mold and forge their own path to success.

Take, for instance, the story of **Lakshmi**, a young woman from a small village in rural India. Her family expected her to follow in the footsteps of her elder sister, getting married young and dedicating her life to domestic duties. But Lakshmi had other dreams. She yearned to escape the confines of her village and pursue an education. Despite facing immense resistance from her family and community, Lakshmi persevered, studying diligently and eventually earning a degree in medicine. She became a doctor, serving her community and challenging the traditional expectations placed upon women in her village.

Her story is a testament to the power of courage and determination in the face of societal pressures. Lakshmi's journey demonstrates that it is possible to defy expectations and live a life that is true to oneself.

The Power of Self-Definition

Redefining success is not about rejecting societal norms or abandoning our cultural heritage. It is about embracing our individuality, our unique talents, and our personal dreams. It is about finding a balance between respecting tradition and honoring our own aspirations.

Each individual has the power to define their own path to success. It is a journey of self-discovery, of identifying our core values and passions, and of pursuing a life that aligns with these values. We can find success in a wide range of pursuits, from artistic expression to scientific discovery, from entrepreneurship to community activism.

Crafting Our Own Narratives

Redefining success is also about crafting our own narratives. We can no longer allow society to dictate our stories, to define our achievements and failures. We must reclaim our power to write our own narratives, to tell our own stories on our own terms.

This journey of crafting our own narratives starts with introspection, with examining our beliefs, values, and aspirations. It involves recognizing the impact of societal pressures and questioning the assumptions we have inherited. It is a process of self-awareness and self-acceptance.

As we craft our narratives, we must embrace our vulnerabilities and imperfections. We must acknowledge that we are not perfect, that we will make mistakes, and that we will face setbacks along the way. These experiences are not failures but opportunities for learning and growth.

Finding Our Own Meaning

The journey of redefining success is not about achieving external validation or conforming to societal expectations. It is about finding meaning and purpose in our own lives. It is about living a life that is aligned with our values, our passions, and our authentic selves.

This journey can be challenging, requiring us to step outside our comfort zones, to confront our fears, and to embrace the unknown. But it is a journey worth taking, a journey that leads to a life of freedom, fulfillment, and authenticity.

The Journey Ahead

Redefining success is an ongoing journey, a lifelong pursuit of self-discovery and personal growth. It is a journey that requires courage, resilience, and a willingness to embrace change. As we navigate this journey, it is essential to surround ourselves with supportive individuals who believe in our potential and encourage us to live our lives authentically.

We must also remember that success is not a destination but a process, a continuous evolution of our beliefs, values, and aspirations. It is about living a life that is true to us, a life that reflects our unique talents and passions.

The journey of redefining success is a journey of self-discovery, a journey of breaking free from the constraints of societal expectations, and a journey of living a life that is truly our own. It is a journey that will lead us to a life of fulfillment, authenticity, and joy.

<u>Crafting a Personal Narrative:</u>

The weight of expectations is a constant companion in the lives of many Indians. It's a force that can feel as heavy as a mountain, a tapestry woven from the threads of societal norms, familial traditions, and personal aspirations. It whispers in our ears, suggesting paths we should follow, roles we should play, and achievements we should strive for. While these expectations can sometimes act as guiding stars, they often become constraints, shaping our choices and limiting our perspectives.

This chapter delves into the complex world of expectations, exploring how they are formed, how they influence us, and most importantly, how we can break free from their hold. We will embark on a journey of self-discovery, questioning the expectations we inherit, recognizing their impact on our lives, and ultimately, reclaiming the power to define our own paths.

The first step in this journey is to understand the origins of these expectations. They are often deeply rooted in our cultural heritage, shaped by generations of traditions, beliefs, and societal values. In Indian culture, family plays a central role, and expectations often stem from a desire to uphold family honor, ensure social acceptance, and fulfill the dreams that have been passed down through generations. From a young age, we are taught what constitutes a "successful" life, often measured in terms of education, career, marriage, and the acquisition of material possessions. These expectations can be both empowering and stifling, offering guidance while simultaneously constricting our sense of individuality.

The pressure to conform to these expectations can be immense, leading individuals to suppress their own desires and ambitions in pursuit of fulfilling external expectations. The fear of disappointing loved ones, the yearning for societal approval, and the ingrained belief that certain paths are preordained can create a sense of obligation and responsibility that feels insurmountable. The weight of expectations can manifest in various forms, from subtle suggestions to overt pressures.

The journey of breaking free from these expectations is not about rejecting our heritage or disregarding the love and guidance of our families. Instead, it is about embracing the freedom to define our own path, to explore our passions, and to live a life that is authentically ours. It requires a shift in perspective, a willingness to challenge the societal norms that have been ingrained in us, and a commitment to forging our own identity.

This chapter encourages you to embark on a profound journey of self-reflection. It invites you to explore the expectations that have shaped your life, to understand their origins, and to assess their impact on your choices, your aspirations, and your overall sense of well-being. Through this exploration, you will gain a deeper understanding of yourself, your values, and your potential.

To embark on this transformative journey, let's delve into a series of exercises designed to help you unravel the weight of expectations and rewrite your own narrative.

Exercise 1: Mapping the Expectations

Step 1: Grab a pen and paper or open a new document on your computer. Create a table with two columns. Label the first column "Source of Expectation" and the second column "Specific Expectation".

Step 2: Think about the major sources of expectations in your life, such as family, culture, religion, society, friends, or your own personal aspirations. List these sources in the first column of your table.

Step 3: For each source, list the specific expectations that you have internalized. These could be related to education, career, marriage, family, social behavior, financial success, or any other area of your life. Be honest and thorough in capturing these expectations.

Exercise 2: Exploring the Impact

Step 1: Take a close look at the list of expectations you have identified. For each expectation, ask yourself the following questions:

Does this expectation bring me joy and fulfillment, or does it create stress and anxiety?

Does it align with my values and aspirations, or does it feel like an external imposition?

Does it inspire me to grow and learn, or does it hold me back from exploring new possibilities?

Step 2: Reflect on your responses to these questions. Identify any expectations that are causing you to feel burdened, restricted, or unfulfilled. Acknowledge the impact of these expectations on your emotional well-being, your decision-making, and your overall sense of purpose.

Exercise 3: Rewriting Your Narrative

Step 1: Consider the expectations that you have identified as limiting or burdensome. For each of these expectations, ask yourself:

What is the story that I am telling myself about this expectation? Is it based on facts or on assumptions?

What would happen if I chose to challenge or redefine this expectation?

What are my own personal aspirations and desires in this area of my life?

Step 2: Start rewriting your narrative. Replace the expectations that no longer serve you with your own values, aspirations, and dreams. Embrace the freedom to choose your own path, to define success on your own terms, and to pursue a life that is authentically yours.

Stories of Defiance

As you embark on this journey of rewriting your narrative, it can be incredibly inspiring to hear the stories of individuals who have defied expectations and carved their own path. These stories remind us that the weight of expectations can be overcome, that we have the power to choose a different course, and that the journey of self-discovery can be both exhilarating and empowering.

Consider the story of **Maya**, a young woman from a traditional Indian family who was expected to pursue a career in medicine or law. However, Maya's heart belonged to the arts. She had a passion for music, a gift for storytelling, and a desire to create something beautiful. Despite the resistance from her family, she pursued her passion, studied music, and eventually, became a renowned singer and songwriter. Maya's journey reminds us that it is possible to defy expectations, to follow our own passions, and to create a life that is both fulfilling and meaningful.

Another inspiring story is that of **Raj**, a young man who grew up in a small village in India, where the expectation was for him to follow in his father's footsteps and become a farmer. Raj, however, had a thirst for knowledge and a dream of studying engineering. He persevered, earned a scholarship to study in the city, and eventually became a successful software engineer. Raj's story reminds us that it is never too late to break free from limitations, to pursue our dreams, and to create a future that is brighter than what we were told was possible.

These stories are not just tales of individual triumph; they are testaments to the power of resilience, the courage to challenge the status quo, and the unwavering belief in the possibility of creating a life that is true to us. They inspire us to look beyond the weight of expectations, to embrace our own unique potential, and to write our own stories, one courageous step at a time.

The Journey of Transformation

Breaking free from the weight of expectations is not a one-time event; it is a lifelong journey of transformation. It requires ongoing self-reflection, a willingness to learn and grow, and a commitment to staying true to ourselves. It is a journey of recognizing our own values, embracing our own passions, and defining success on our own terms.

As you embark on this journey, remember that you are not alone. Surround yourself with a supportive network of family, friends, and mentors who believe in you and encourage your growth. Seek out resources and support systems that help you navigate the challenges of breaking free from societal norms and pursuing your own path. And most importantly, be patient with yourself. The journey of self-discovery is a process, and it takes time to understand ourselves, to challenge our beliefs, and to redefine our expectations.

The journey of rewriting your narrative is not about abandoning your heritage or ignoring the love and guidance of your family. It is about reclaiming your power, embracing your individuality, and creating a life that is authentically yours. It is about living beyond the brackets, embracing the infinite possibilities that life offers, and writing your own story, a story of self-discovery, empowerment, and fulfillment.

3

THE POWER OF BELIEF SYSTEMS

Origins of Beliefs:

The origins of our beliefs, the bedrock of our perspectives, are a fascinating tapestry woven from the threads of our experiences, the voices that surround us, and the stories we tell ourselves. These beliefs, often formed unconsciously, shape our worldviews, influencing our choices, actions, and even the very way we perceive reality. Like invisible guides, they steer us toward certain paths while discouraging others, becoming the architects of our lives, both for better and for worse.

Imagine a young girl growing up in a small village in rural India. Surrounded by a community where everyone seems to follow the same traditions and pursue the same dreams, she absorbs these societal norms as unquestionable truths. She witnesses her mother toiling tirelessly within the confines of their home, dedicating her life to caring for the family. She observes her father, a farmer, working tirelessly under the scorching sun, barely able to make ends meet. This world, her world, becomes the only reality she knows.

As she grows, she internalizes the messages she receives from her family, her community, and the wider society. "Girls should be good wives and mothers," her grandmother whispers, her words carrying the weight of generations. "Education is for boys, not for girls," her father declares, his words echoing the prevailing sentiment in their village. These messages, repeated over and over, gradually become ingrained in her psyche, forming the very foundation of her belief system.

The seeds of belief are sown early, often in the fertile soil of childhood. The stories we hear, the lessons we learn, and the experiences we encounter shape our understanding of the world. We internalize the values and norms of our families, our communities, and the wider society, shaping our perceptions and defining our sense of self. The unquestioned truths of our childhood, often passed down through generations, become the invisible walls that confine us, limiting our choices and influencing our destinies.

Consider the impact of cultural norms on our beliefs. In many Indian households, the expectation of arranged marriages still holds considerable sway. This belief, passed down through generations, becomes a cornerstone in the lives of many individuals. Some embrace it wholeheartedly, finding solace and security in the traditional path. Others, however, struggle with its constraints, yearning for a love that goes beyond societal expectations. The beliefs we inherit, whether cultural, religious, or familial, act as powerful lenses through which we view the world, shaping our choices and our lives.

But the tapestry of beliefs is not woven solely from inherited wisdom. Our personal experiences, both joyous and painful, contribute to the intricate patterns that form our belief systems. A child who is praised and encouraged for her academic achievements may develop a strong belief in her abilities, paving the way for a successful career. Conversely, a child who is constantly criticized or ridiculed may internalize a belief of inadequacy, affecting their self-esteem and their willingness to take risks. Each experience, every interaction, leaves its mark, shaping the fabric of our beliefs.

Furthermore, the information we consume through various media outlets, from books and television to the internet and social media, further enriches the tapestry of our beliefs. The narratives we encounter, the ideas we absorb, and the perspectives we are exposed to all contribute to the ever-evolving landscape of our beliefs. This information, though seemingly detached from our personal experiences, can profoundly influence our worldviews, shaping our opinions and influencing our actions.

The influence of social media, in particular, has become a defining factor in shaping our beliefs in the modern era. The constant stream of information, images, and opinions can create a powerful sense of interconnectedness, yet it can also lead to the formation of echo chambers, where individuals are primarily exposed to views that confirm their existing beliefs, reinforcing biases and deepening divides.

The power of belief systems lies in their ability to shape our perceptions of ourselves and the world around us. They determine how we interpret events, how we interact with others, and how we navigate the complexities of life. Our beliefs, like the threads of a tapestry, are woven together, forming a complex and intricate pattern that defines our unique worldview.

However, the power of belief systems can also be their downfall. When our beliefs are rigid and inflexible, they can act as barriers, hindering our growth, limiting our potential, and preventing us from embracing new possibilities. Our beliefs, like the comfort zones they often reinforce, can trap us within the familiar, preventing us from venturing into the unknown, from exploring new horizons, from truly living life to its fullest.

It is crucial to recognize that beliefs are not immutable truths but rather interpretations based on our experiences and perspectives. They can be challenged, questioned, and even transformed. The journey of personal growth often involves questioning our deeply held beliefs, examining their origins, and assessing their impact on our lives. It is a process of self-discovery, of shedding limiting beliefs and embracing empowering ones, of opening ourselves to new possibilities and expanding our horizons.

The exploration of our belief systems is a journey of self-reflection, a quest for deeper understanding and self-acceptance. It is a process of recognizing how our beliefs have shaped our lives, both consciously and unconsciously. Through this introspective journey, we can identify limiting beliefs that hold us back, beliefs that have been ingrained in us through societal expectations, cultural norms, or personal experiences. We can then challenge these beliefs, questioning their validity, their impact, and their relevance to our lives.

One of the most powerful tools for transforming our beliefs is through the art of storytelling. Stories have the power to challenge our assumptions, expand our perspectives, and awaken our imaginations. By encountering diverse narratives, stories that offer different perspectives and challenge our own worldviews, we begin to see the world through new lenses, opening ourselves to new possibilities and dismantling rigid beliefs.

The power of storytelling lies in its ability to connect with our emotions, to create empathy, and to foster understanding. Through the shared experiences of others, we can gain insights into ourselves, recognizing our own biases and challenging our preconceived notions. By embracing the power of storytelling, we open ourselves to the transformative potential of new ideas and perspectives, paving the way for personal growth and a more fulfilling life.

In the next chapter, we will explore the role of limiting beliefs in shaping our life choices. We will examine how these beliefs, often formed early in life, can create invisible barriers that restrict our potential and limit our opportunities. We will then delve into strategies for challenging these limiting beliefs, reclaiming our power, and creating lives that are aligned with our deepest aspirations. The journey of transformation begins with a willingness to question, to challenge, and to re-evaluate the beliefs that have defined us, paving the way for a life of greater purpose, fulfillment, and limitless possibilities.

Beliefs as Barriers:

The invisible shackles of our beliefs, often formed in the crucible of childhood experiences, societal pressures, and cultural norms, can act as potent barriers to personal growth and fulfilling lives. These beliefs, though seemingly harmless, can subtly shape our perceptions, influencing our decisions, relationships, and overall worldview. They can be like invisible walls, limiting our potential and keeping us tethered to a constricted version of ourselves.

Imagine a young woman named **Rani**, raised in a traditional Indian family, where the expectation for women was to prioritize marriage and family over personal ambitions. Rani, gifted with a sharp intellect and a passion for science, internalized this belief, believing that her calling lay within the domestic sphere. As she excelled in her studies, the whispers of doubt began to surface, questioning her aspirations and urging her to prioritize a stable marriage. This internal conflict, fueled by her ingrained beliefs, led her to suppress her desires and choose a comfortable, yet unfulfilling path, accepting a career in a traditional field to appease societal expectations.

This is a story echoed in countless lives, where deeply rooted beliefs, often passed down through generations, become ingrained in our psyche, acting as invisible filters through which we view the world. These limiting beliefs, like the societal pressure Rani faced, can dictate our choices, shaping our careers, relationships, and overall happiness. They can become self-fulfilling prophecies, hindering our ability to explore our potential and embrace the richness that life has to offer.

Let's examine the insidious nature of these limiting beliefs, starting with the seemingly innocuous, "I'm not good at math." This belief, often rooted in early childhood experiences, can impact a child's confidence in STEM subjects, leading to avoidance of these fields and potentially limiting future career options. Similarly, beliefs like "I'm not creative" or "I'm not meant for leadership" can stifle the exploration of artistic talents or stifle ambitions to lead.

These beliefs are not merely intellectual constructs; they are emotionally charged, often forming a foundation for our self-image and sense of self-worth. They can become deeply ingrained, leading to feelings of inadequacy or fear of failure, further reinforcing these negative beliefs. The impact of these limiting beliefs transcends individual lives, perpetuating societal inequalities and hindering progress.

Take, for example, the belief that women are less capable than men in leadership roles. This belief, fueled by historical and societal biases, can have a profound impact on women's career paths, leading to limited opportunities and unequal pay. This ingrained belief, coupled with societal expectations of women's roles, can create a vicious cycle of self-doubt and underachievement, ultimately restricting women's potential and hindering their progress.

The insidious nature of these limiting beliefs lies in their often-unconscious influence on our actions and reactions. We may not even be aware of the impact they have on our daily lives, yet they subtly influence our decisions, dictating our choices, and shaping our reality.

Recognizing the existence of these limiting beliefs is the first step towards breaking free from their grip. Self-awareness is the key to understanding how these beliefs, shaped by our experiences, societal norms, and cultural influences, have shaped our perspectives. Once we become conscious of these ingrained beliefs, we can begin to question their validity, challenging their influence on our lives.

Challenging these beliefs is not about discarding them entirely but rather about recognizing their influence and actively seeking alternative perspectives. Engaging in critical self-reflection, questioning the source of these beliefs, and seeking out diverse viewpoints can help us develop a more nuanced and objective understanding of ourselves and the world. This process, though challenging, can lead to a more liberating and authentic way of living.

Remember, Rani, with her ingrained belief in the limitations of her gender, could have chosen to challenge this belief, seeking out mentors and role models who defied societal expectations. She could have explored her passion for science, seeking opportunities to break free from the constraints of societal norms. Her journey could have been one of self-discovery, leading to a fulfilling career and a life lived on her own terms.

The power of belief systems, both empowering and limiting, is undeniable. Recognizing the impact of these beliefs, whether positive or negative, is the first step towards a life lived with intention and purpose. Embracing a more conscious approach to our belief systems can be the catalyst for personal growth, allowing us to break free from self-imposed limitations and embrace the infinite possibilities that lie beyond the confines of our beliefs.

<u>Challenging Core Beliefs:</u>

The beliefs we hold, those fundamental truths we carry within, are often the invisible architects of our lives. They shape our choices, dictate our actions, and color our perceptions of the world. While some beliefs serve as guiding stars, leading us towards fulfilling lives, others can act as shackles, limiting our potential and keeping us trapped within self-imposed boundaries. This chapter delves into the fascinating realm of belief systems, exploring how they are formed, how they influence our lives, and most importantly, how we can challenge and transform those beliefs that no longer serve us.

Imagine a tightly woven tapestry, each thread representing a belief we hold dear. Some threads are strong and resilient, representing beliefs that have stood the test of time and shaped our values. Others, however, might be frayed and brittle, reflecting beliefs that are outdated, limiting, or even harmful. It is within this tapestry of beliefs that we navigate the complexities of our lives.

The origins of our beliefs are diverse, often stemming from a combination of experiences, upbringing, cultural influences, and even inherited societal norms. From a young age, we are bombarded with messages and narratives that shape our understanding of the world. We observe the actions of our parents, absorb the teachings of our elders, and internalize the values of our community. These experiences weave themselves into the fabric of our beliefs, shaping our perceptions, attitudes, and ultimately, our choices.

However, the power of belief systems lies not just in their formation but also in their influence on our actions. Our beliefs act as filters, influencing how we interpret information, respond to challenges, and even perceive ourselves. If we hold the belief that we are not capable of achieving something, it's more likely we'll avoid that goal altogether, even unconsciously sabotaging ourselves. Conversely, a belief in our own potential can empower us to overcome obstacles and achieve extraordinary things.

The insidious nature of limiting beliefs lies in their subtle yet profound influence. They often operate beneath the surface of our consciousness, shaping our choices and actions without us fully recognizing their impact. We might find ourselves repeating patterns of behavior that are no longer serving us, or we might struggle to break free from relationships or situations that are clearly unhealthy. These recurring patterns are often a reflection of limiting beliefs that are holding us back.

Consider the common belief that "money is the root of all evil." While this phrase holds some truth, it can easily become a limiting belief, hindering individuals from pursuing financial stability and success. They might avoid taking risks, settle for jobs they dislike, or even view wealth as something to be ashamed of. This belief, rooted in fear and negativity, can lead to a life of poverty and missed opportunities.

The question then becomes, how can we effectively challenge and alter these limiting beliefs? The process of transforming our belief systems is not a quick fix, but a journey of self-discovery and conscious evolution. It involves a willingness to question our assumptions, confront our fears, and embrace a new way of seeing the world.

Here are some strategies that can help you embark on this transformative journey:

1. Become Aware of Your Beliefs: The first step is to identify the beliefs you hold. Take some time for introspection, reflecting on your thoughts, actions, and reactions to various situations. Ask yourself: "What do I believe about myself? What do I believe about the world? What do I believe about success, relationships, money, and happiness?" Be honest with yourself and don't shy away from beliefs that feel uncomfortable or challenging.

2. Question Your Beliefs: Once you've identified your beliefs, it's time to question them. Ask yourself: "Where did this belief come from? Is it truly true? Is it serving me? Are there alternative perspectives I haven't considered?" Challenge the assumptions that underpin your beliefs and seek out evidence that might contradict them.

3. Examine the Evidence: For every belief you hold, there's likely a story or a set of experiences that supports it. However, it's crucial to examine the evidence objectively. Are you relying on anecdotal evidence, personal biases, or outdated information? Look for credible sources and diverse perspectives that might challenge your assumptions.

4. Seek Out Different Perspectives: One of the most effective ways to challenge limiting beliefs is to expose yourself to diverse perspectives. Talk to people from different backgrounds, cultures, and walks of life. Read books, watch documentaries, and immerse yourself in different viewpoints. By broadening your understanding of the world, you'll gain a more nuanced and objective perspective on your own beliefs.

5. Practice Mindfulness: Mindfulness is the key to becoming more aware of your own thoughts and beliefs. Through meditation, deep breathing exercises, or simply paying attention to your breath, you can learn to observe your thoughts without judgment. This practice allows you to identify limiting beliefs as they arise and challenge them with a more mindful and compassionate approach.

6. Engage in Positive Affirmations: Affirmations are positive statements that can help reprogram your subconscious mind. By repeating affirmations regularly, you can gradually replace negative beliefs with positive ones. For example, instead of believing, "I'm not good enough," you could affirm, "I am capable, worthy, and deserving of success."

7. Surround Yourself with Supportive People: Our social circles significantly influence our beliefs. If you're surrounded by people who reinforce limiting beliefs, it's time to expand your network. Seek out individuals who challenge your perspective, inspire you to grow, and support your journey of personal transformation.

8. Embrace the Power of Storytelling: Our stories, both the ones we tell ourselves and the ones we hear from others, shape our beliefs. Pay attention to the narratives you internalize and the stories you tell yourself. Are they empowering you to move forward or holding you back? If you notice limiting narratives, work towards replacing them with empowering stories that align with your desired future.

Remember, challenging your core beliefs is not about erasing your past or abandoning your identity. It's about expanding your perspective, embracing new possibilities, and creating a life that reflects your true values and aspirations. The journey of belief transformation can be challenging, but it can also be deeply rewarding, leading you to a life that is more fulfilling, authentic, and aligned with your highest potential.

Transformative Stories of Change:

The power of beliefs is a profound force that shapes our realities. Often, we don't even realize the extent to which our beliefs govern our thoughts, actions, and ultimately, our lives. These deeply ingrained convictions, formed through personal experiences, societal influences, and cultural norms, become invisible frameworks that guide our perceptions and choices.

In India, a land steeped in tradition and cultural values, the impact of beliefs is particularly potent. From the age-old wisdom passed down through generations to the modern-day influences of media and social structures, our beliefs are a tapestry woven with threads of cultural norms, societal expectations, and individual experiences.

While beliefs can serve as pillars of stability and guide us toward fulfilling lives, they can also act as barriers, limiting our potential and preventing us from realizing our dreams. This is where the transformative power of challenging our beliefs comes into play. It's about recognizing those beliefs that might be holding us back, questioning their validity, and ultimately, choosing to embrace new, empowering perspectives.

Let's delve into the lives of individuals who have dared to confront their limiting beliefs and emerge transformed.

Avani's Journey: Breaking the Cycle of Fear

Avani, a young woman from a conservative family in Delhi, grew up with the belief that her primary role in life was to get married and raise a family. Her parents, like many in their community, held a strong belief in arranged marriages, seeing them as the safest and most secure path to happiness. As Avani navigated her teenage years, this belief became ingrained in her own psyche, creating a sense of obligation and a fear of defying societal norms.

"I was constantly being reminded that I was destined for this path, that my life was pre-determined. The fear of disappointing my family, of being ostracized by our community, was a constant shadow that followed me," Avani shared during a workshop on self-discovery.

However, Avani harbored a secret ambition – a burning desire to pursue higher education and build a career in science. This dream clashed head-on with the deeply ingrained belief system she had inherited. The fear of rebellion, the fear of judgment, and the fear of sacrificing her family's expectations weighed heavily on her.

One fateful day, Avani stumbled upon a workshop on self-discovery, a catalyst that ignited a spark of courage within her. The workshop exposed her to the power of challenging limiting beliefs and the importance of pursuing one's passions. It opened her eyes to the possibility of a life lived on her own terms, a life where personal fulfillment could coexist with family responsibilities.

Inspired by the workshop, Avani began a journey of self-reflection and introspection. She started questioning her beliefs, analyzing their origins and their impact on her life. The more she explored, the more she realized that her fear was not rooted in reality but in a perception shaped by societal norms.

With newfound clarity, Avani decided to take a leap of faith. She confessed her dream to her parents, bracing herself for their disapproval. To her surprise, her parents, while initially taken aback, were moved by her passion and determination. They had always nurtured her intellect and encouraged her pursuits, but the societal pressure to conform had blinded them to Avani's own aspirations.

Avani's story is a testament to the power of challenging limiting beliefs. It shows how fear, often rooted in societal expectations, can hinder our dreams. By confronting her ingrained beliefs and daring to embrace a different path, Avani not only unlocked her own potential but also sparked a conversation within her family, challenging traditional notions about women's roles in society.

Mehul's Transformation: Breaking the Cycle of Conformity

Mehul, a young man from a middle-class family in Mumbai, grew up believing that a successful life meant pursuing a stable career, acquiring material possessions, and securing a comfortable future. His father, a businessman, had always instilled in him the importance of hard work, financial security, and social status. Mehul, influenced by these values, excelled in his studies, securing a coveted engineering degree. However, deep within him, a flicker of discontent began to grow.

While he achieved success in his career, Mehul found himself yearning for something more fulfilling. His job, though financially rewarding, lacked a sense of purpose and felt uninspiring. He felt a disconnect between his work and his true passions, which lay in the realm of art and music.

Mehul's journey to liberation began when he stumbled upon an article about mindfulness and self-discovery. It sparked a deep introspection, forcing him to confront the disconnect between his outward achievements and his inner desires. The article challenged the conventional notion of success, suggesting that true fulfillment lay in aligning one's actions with one's passions and values.

Inspired by these ideas, Mehul began exploring his artistic side. He enrolled in painting classes, reconnected with his love for music, and started expressing himself through various creative outlets. At first, the fear of judgment and the pressure to conform weighed on him. He grappled with the uncertainty of abandoning a secure career path, the potential disapproval of his family, and the societal stigma attached to pursuing unconventional pursuits.

However, Mehul's desire for authenticity and self-expression proved stronger than his fear. He gradually opened up to his family about his artistic aspirations, sharing his anxieties and hopes. To his surprise, his parents, who had always encouraged his academic pursuits, showed understanding and support. They realized that true happiness for Mehul lay in pursuing his passion, even if it meant stepping outside of the conventional paths they had envisioned for him.

Mehul's journey serves as an inspiring example of how challenging, limiting beliefs can lead to a more fulfilling life. By breaking free from the societal pressure to conform, by embracing his true self and pursuing his artistic passion, Mehul redefined success on his own terms, demonstrating that a life lived authentically is a life worth living.

Rekha's Redemption: Embracing a New Narrative

Rekha, a middle-aged woman from a village in Rajasthan, lived a life defined by societal expectations and traditional roles. Growing up, she witnessed her mother tirelessly managing the household, sacrificing her own aspirations for the well-being of her family. Rekha, influenced by these societal norms, accepted her fate, believing that her life was destined to follow a similar trajectory.

She married young, raised a family, and dedicated herself to the responsibilities of a traditional Indian homemaker. However, within the confines of this seemingly fulfilling life, Rekha harbored a secret longing – a yearning for education and a sense of personal accomplishment.

Rekha's journey of transformation began with a simple act of kindness. A local teacher, noticing her inquisitive nature and thirst for knowledge, offered her free literacy classes. As Rekha learned to read and write, a new world opened up to her. It ignited a desire for further education and a longing to break free from the limitations of her traditional role.

This newfound knowledge sparked a conversation with her husband, a conversation that challenged the ingrained beliefs they both held about a woman's place in society. While he initially hesitated, his love and respect for Rekha, combined with the realization of her potential, led him to support her aspirations.

Rekha's journey took a dramatic turn when she enrolled in an evening program at the local community college. She faced numerous challenges, from societal stigma to juggling household responsibilities with her studies. However, her determination was unshakable, fueled by a newfound belief in her own capabilities and a desire to create a better life for herself and her family.

Rekha's story exemplifies the power of challenging limiting beliefs and embracing new narratives. It's a powerful testament to the transformative power of education, not just in acquiring knowledge but also in empowering individuals to challenge societal norms and create their own destinies. Rekha's journey is a reminder that it's never too late to break free from the confines of traditional expectations and embrace the possibilities of personal growth and self-discovery.

Embracing the Power of Belief

The narratives of Avani, Mehul, and Rekha demonstrate the profound impact of beliefs on our lives. They highlight the power of challenging limiting beliefs, of questioning the narratives we have inherited, and of embracing new perspectives that empower us to create a life of fulfillment and purpose.

The journey of transforming beliefs is not always easy. It often involves facing fears, confronting societal pressures, and navigating challenges. However, the rewards are immeasurable, leading to personal growth, self-discovery, and a life lived authentically.

As we embark on our own journeys of self-discovery, let us be inspired by the courage of those who have dared to break free from limiting beliefs. Let their stories serve as a reminder that the power to transform our lives lies within us, within the beliefs we choose to embrace.

Building a New Foundation

The stories shared above are just a glimpse into the vast landscape of human experiences. The transformative power of belief systems transcends individual narratives; it is a universal force that has the potential to shape societies and influence the course of human history.

The journey of transforming beliefs is a lifelong process, a continuous exploration of our own identities and values. It is a journey of self-discovery, of embracing new perspectives, and of forging a path that aligns with our true selves.

As we move forward, let us commit to:

Consciously examining our beliefs: What are the beliefs we hold? Where do they originate? Are they serving us or holding us back?

Questioning ingrained narratives: Are there any societal norms or expectations that we have internalized without questioning their validity? How can we challenge those narratives that limit our potential?

Cultivating an open mind: Embrace diverse perspectives, listen with empathy, and seek to understand the world through different lenses.

Embracing personal growth: Make a conscious effort to challenge our limiting beliefs and embrace new, empowering perspectives.

Supporting others on their journeys: Encourage and support those around us as they navigate their own journeys of self-discovery and belief transformation.

The power of belief systems is a force that can either restrict or empower. By embracing the transformative power of questioning and changing our beliefs, we can unlock a world of possibilities, creating a life of purpose, authenticity, and fulfillment.

Embracing New Perspectives:

The power of belief systems is deeply intertwined with our lived experiences. They shape our choices, guide our actions, and define our perceptions of the world. These beliefs are not just abstract notions; they are powerful forces that influence every aspect of our lives.

Imagine a young woman named **Mira**, a talented artist struggling to find her voice amidst societal expectations. She was raised in a family that valued traditional professions like medicine or engineering. Her parents, well-meaning but deeply rooted in societal norms, constantly encouraged her to pursue a stable career, one that promised security and social recognition. However, Mira's heart belonged to the vibrant world of colors and canvases. Despite her inherent artistic talent, she struggled with crippling self-doubt, questioning if her passion was a viable path.

The weight of these inherited beliefs, ingrained by her family and societal pressure, created a barrier between Mira and her dream. She believed that pursuing art would be considered a failure, a deviation from the expected trajectory. She doubted her abilities, convinced that she didn't have what it took to make it as an artist. These limiting beliefs, nurtured by years of ingrained societal expectations, held her captive, preventing her from pursuing her passion.

Now, let's shift our focus to another individual, Ram, a young man battling the societal stigma associated with mental health issues. Ram, a bright and ambitious engineer, faced a breakdown after a particularly stressful project. He felt overwhelmed, burdened by the pressure to succeed in a demanding corporate environment. However, seeking help for his mental health felt like a weakness, a sign of failure. Ram had grown up in a culture where mental health was considered taboo, a topic not to be discussed. He feared judgment, the social isolation that often accompanies vulnerability. He believed that seeking professional help would make him appear weak and unworthy, reinforcing the stigma he had internalized.

Mira and Ram's stories highlight the powerful impact of limiting beliefs. These beliefs, often formed through years of cultural conditioning, societal norms, and personal experiences, can act as invisible barriers, holding us back from reaching our full potential. They can create self-doubt, hinder decision-making, and even limit our capacity for joy and fulfillment.

The good news is that we have the power to challenge these limiting beliefs and replace them with empowering ones. This journey of transformation requires introspection, awareness, and a willingness to embrace new perspectives.

Let's delve into the process of identifying and challenging these beliefs. The first step is to become aware of our own belief systems. What do we believe about ourselves, our capabilities, and the world around us? Are these beliefs helping or hindering our growth?

To gain clarity, it's important to introspect and observe our thoughts. Pay attention to our internal dialogue, the recurring thoughts, and assumptions that shape our perceptions. We can use a simple journaling exercise to explore our beliefs:

> **Identify Limiting Beliefs:** Reflect on areas where you feel stuck or limited. Are there any recurring negative thoughts about yourself or your abilities? What are the beliefs that are holding you back? Write them down. For instance, "I'm not good enough," "I'm not smart enough," or "I'm not worthy of success," are common

limiting beliefs that can restrict our growth.

Challenge Those Beliefs: Once you've identified limiting beliefs, question their validity. Ask yourself: where did these beliefs come from? Are they truly accurate? What evidence supports them? What evidence contradicts them? The process of questioning and challenging these beliefs can be a powerful step toward dismantling them.

Rewrite Your Narrative: Replace limiting beliefs with empowering ones. For instance, if you struggle with a belief like "I'm not worthy of success," challenge it by asking, "What makes me unworthy? What evidence supports this belief?" Replace this negative belief with a more positive one like "I am capable of achieving success" or "I deserve happiness and fulfillment."

Focus on What You Can Control: Recognize that you have the power to shape your thoughts and beliefs. You can choose to focus on the positive, on your strengths, and on the possibilities that lie ahead.

The process of challenging and changing beliefs is an ongoing journey, not a one-time event. It requires conscious effort, mindfulness, and a commitment to personal growth.

Here are some strategies that can help you embrace new perspectives:

Surround Yourself with Positive Influences: Seek out individuals who challenge your limiting beliefs and inspire you to think differently. Engage in conversations that expand your horizons and expose you to diverse perspectives.

Read Empowering Books: Immerse yourself in books that challenge societal norms, question limiting beliefs, and offer alternative viewpoints.

Embrace Personal Growth Activities: Participate in workshops, seminars, or online courses that focus on personal growth, self-discovery, and positive psychology.

Seek Professional Guidance: If you struggle to challenge deeply ingrained beliefs, consider seeking the support of a therapist or counselor. They can provide a safe space to explore your beliefs, develop coping mechanisms, and work towards positive change.

Practice Gratitude: Take time each day to focus on the good things in your life. Practice gratitude for your strengths, your accomplishments, and the support you receive. Gratitude can shift your focus from negativity to positivity, fostering a more optimistic outlook.

Remember, changing your beliefs is a powerful act of self-empowerment. It's about taking control of your thoughts and choices, shaping your own narrative, and moving forward with greater confidence and clarity. The journey may not be easy, but the rewards – a life filled with purpose, joy, and fulfillment – are worth every step.

4

THE COURAGE TO CHANGE

<u>Understanding Fear and Change:</u>

Fear, a primal instinct that has kept us safe from predators and danger for millennia, can also become a powerful force that holds us back from growth and change. The fear of the unknown, the fear of failure, the fear of judgment – these are the invisible shackles that bind us to our comfort zones, preventing us from embracing new opportunities and living lives filled with purpose and fulfillment.

Change, by its very nature, is inherently disruptive. It challenges our familiar routines, our deeply held beliefs, and our comfortable sense of certainty. The fear of change, therefore, is not irrational; it's a natural human response to the perceived threat of disruption. Yet, clinging to the comfort of the familiar can be a far greater threat to our well-being in the long run.

Imagine a tree rooted in the same patch of soil, never exposed to the elements, never reaching for the sun. Its branches might be lush and green, but they would be stunted, fragile, and ultimately unable to withstand the force of a strong wind. We, too, can become trapped in this state of arrested development if we allow fear to dictate our choices.

In the context of our lives, the fear of change can manifest itself in various ways. It might stop us from pursuing a new career path, despite our passion for it, because of the perceived risk of failure. It might prevent us from speaking up for what we believe in, fearing the disapproval of those around us. Or it might hold us back from expressing our true selves, out of fear of being judged or rejected.

However, the fear of change is not insurmountable. It is a powerful emotion, but it is not an all-powerful force. We have the ability to understand its roots, to confront it with courage, and to ultimately overcome it.

One of the first steps in confronting fear is to acknowledge its presence. Instead of trying to ignore or suppress it, we must recognize it for what it is: a signal that something new and challenging is about to occur. We must learn to differentiate between fear that is based on real danger and fear that is based on our own assumptions and anxieties.

Once we have acknowledged our fear, we can begin to understand it. What are the specific things that we are afraid of? What are the worst-case scenarios that we are imagining? By examining our fears more closely, we can start to see them for what they are: often exaggerated, irrational, and ultimately based on our own insecurities.

Another crucial step is to develop our resilience. Resilience is the ability to bounce back from setbacks, to learn from our mistakes, and to keep going even when things get tough. Building resilience involves developing a strong sense of self-belief, cultivating our emotional intelligence, and learning to adapt to changing circumstances.

Resilience is not about being fearless; it's about learning to navigate fear effectively. It's about recognizing that failure is not the end, but rather a learning opportunity. It's about developing the mental and emotional strength to face challenges head-on and to emerge from them stronger.

We must also learn to differentiate between calculated risks and reckless behavior. Not all change is good, and not all risks are worth taking. Carefully evaluating the potential benefits and drawbacks of a particular change can help us to make informed decisions, minimizing the possibility of regret and maximizing the chances of success.

Creating a support system can also be invaluable in navigating fear and change. Surrounding ourselves with people who believe in us, who offer encouragement and advice, and who are willing to listen to our concerns can make a significant difference in our ability to overcome fear and embrace new possibilities.

Ultimately, the journey of overcoming fear and change is a personal one. Each individual will face unique challenges, and each will find their own path to growth and transformation. But the common thread that connects us all is the courage to step outside of our comfort zones, to confront our fears, and to embrace the endless possibilities that life has to offer.

Consider the story of **Sita**, a young woman living in a small village in India. Sita had always dreamt of becoming a doctor, but her family insisted that she should focus on finding a suitable husband and settling down. Sita, deeply influenced by societal expectations and her family's insistence, had accepted her fate. Yet, a part of her still yearned for something more, for a life that would allow her to fulfill her potential.

One day, a visiting doctor from the city came to Sita's village to provide medical aid. This encounter ignited a spark within Sita. Witnessing the doctor's dedication and compassion, Sita was reminded of her own childhood dream. The fear of defying her family's expectations, the fear of failure, the fear of judgment – all these emotions threatened to hold her back once again. But this time, Sita was determined to fight them.

Armed with unwavering determination, Sita enrolled in a local nursing school. The initial stages were daunting. Her family was disapproving, her friends were skeptical, and she faced the constant weight of societal expectations. However, Sita was supported by a small group of friends who believed in her and her dreams. They encouraged her, helped her to study, and reminded her of the strength and courage she possessed.

Through sheer hard work, dedication, and unwavering resilience, Sita eventually earned her nursing degree. Her story is a testament to the transformative power of change, demonstrating that even when fear looms large, we can overcome it with courage, determination, and belief in ourselves.

The fear of change is a powerful force, but it is not insurmountable. It is through understanding, confronting, and ultimately overcoming fear that we can break free from the invisible shackles that bind us to our comfort zones and embark on journeys of personal growth, fulfillment, and transformation.

<u>Stories of Bravery:</u>

The courage to change is a powerful force, capable of transforming our lives in profound ways. It's the driving force behind personal growth, innovation, and the pursuit of a fulfilling existence. Yet, the fear of the unknown often holds us back, making us cling to the familiar, even if it's no longer serving us. It's in these moments that we must summon bravery to break free from our comfort zones, challenge our beliefs, and embrace the uncertainties that come with change.

The stories of countless individuals who have overcome their fears and embraced change offer a beacon of hope and inspiration. They remind us that even when faced with overwhelming odds, the human spirit is capable of remarkable resilience and transformation.

Take, for instance, the story of Dr. **Pari** Sharma, a rural doctor who left her comfortable life in a bustling city to serve the underserved communities in remote villages. Driven by a deep sense of compassion and a desire to make a difference, she defied societal expectations and risked her own safety to bring healthcare to those who were most in need. Her journey was fraught with challenges, from navigating difficult terrain to confronting cultural prejudices. Yet, she persevered, fueled by a belief in the inherent worth of every human life.

Similarly, consider the story of **Arun** Kumar, a young man who dared to break free from the constraints of his family's expectations and pursue his passion for music. His dream of becoming a musician seemed like a distant fantasy, as his family prioritized a "secure" career path in engineering. However, Arun refused to compromise his dreams. He took the bold step of leaving his engineering program and pursuing music education, facing resistance and disappointment from his family along the way. His dedication and hard work ultimately paid off, leading him to establish himself as a respected musician in the Indian music industry.

These stories serve as powerful testaments to the transformative power of courage. They demonstrate that embracing change, even in the face of fear, can lead to a life of greater purpose, fulfillment, and personal growth. But the journey is rarely smooth. It demands resilience, a willingness to learn from setbacks, and a strong support system.

To navigate the challenges that accompany change, it's essential to understand the nature of fear itself. Fear is an instinctive response that helps us protect ourselves from potential threats. However, it can also become a paralyzing force, preventing us from stepping outside our comfort zones and exploring new possibilities.

When faced with fear, it's crucial to examine its root causes. Is it rooted in past experiences, societal conditioning, or simply a lack of information? By understanding the source of our fears, we can begin to address them head-on.

Building resilience is another crucial step in overcoming fear and embracing change. Resilience is the ability to bounce back from setbacks, adapt to changing circumstances, and maintain a positive outlook. It's a muscle that can be strengthened through various practices, such as mindfulness, gratitude journaling, and seeking out supportive relationships.

Taking calculated risks is an integral part of embracing change. It's not about reckless abandonment, but rather about weighing the potential benefits against the risks involved. Before making a major decision, it's essential to gather information, assess your resources, and consider the potential outcomes. Sometimes, the biggest risks lead to the greatest rewards.

A strong support system is vital in times of change. Surrounding yourself with people who believe in you, encourage your growth, and offer a listening ear can make a world of difference. These individuals can provide emotional support, practical advice, and a safe space to process your fears and anxieties.

Embracing change requires courage, resilience, and a belief in the transformative power of stepping outside our comfort zones. It's a journey that demands honesty, introspection, and a willingness to learn and grow. The stories of those who have dared to embrace change serve as beacons of hope, reminding us that the path to personal fulfillment often lies beyond the boundaries of our fears.

Building Resilience:

The world can be a scary place, especially when we feel like we're about to step outside our comfort zones. Change, even when it promises growth and liberation, can feel like a treacherous path. The fear of the unknown, the worry about failing, the uncertainty of the outcome—these emotions can hold us back, keeping us tethered to the familiar, even if it's not truly serving us anymore. But fear is a powerful force, a potent cocktail of adrenaline and anxiety that can paralyze our courage and dim the light of our dreams.

But what if we could learn to manage this fear, to build a mental resilience that would allow us to embrace change without being consumed by its anxieties? What if we could cultivate a sense of inner strength that would let us walk confidently towards the unknown, knowing that even if we stumble, we have the resources within ourselves to rise again? This is the power of building resilience.

Resilience isn't about being fearless, it's about being brave in the face of fear. It's about learning to acknowledge those anxieties, to understand their origins, and to develop strategies for navigating them. Think of it as building a mental fortress, a strong and sturdy structure that can withstand the onslaught of doubts and anxieties. It's a journey of self-discovery, a process of learning to trust ourselves and our abilities, even when we're unsure about the path ahead.

Building the Foundations of Resilience

The first step in building resilience is understanding the nature of fear. It's a natural human response to perceived threats, a primal instinct that helped our ancestors survive in a dangerous world. Fear can stem from a variety of sources: past experiences, societal conditioning, cultural norms, personal insecurities, and even the simple unknown. Recognizing the roots of our fears is crucial to understanding why we feel anxious in certain situations.

For instance, someone who grew up in a strict household might feel fear around expressing their true self, fearing rejection or disapproval. Another person might be terrified of public speaking, stemming from a childhood experience where they were ridiculed in front of their classmates. In both cases, the fear is rooted in past experiences, shaping their reactions to similar situations in the present.

Unmasking the Fear

The next step is to delve deeper, to unpack the fears themselves. What specific anxieties are we harboring? What are the thoughts that fuel these fears? Are these thoughts rooted in reality or are they simply projections of our own insecurities?

For example, someone might fear a job interview, anticipating rejection. They might worry about being judged, about not being good enough, or about the potential impact of failure on their self-worth. By dissecting these thoughts, we can start to identify the underlying insecurities that are driving the fear.

From Fear to Courage

Once we've identified the source of our fears, we can begin to address them head-on. This is where resilience comes in. Resilience isn't about suppressing our fears, it's about developing a way to navigate them. It's about learning to manage our anxiety so that it doesn't paralyze us, but instead empowers us to act despite our fears.

This can be a challenging process, but it's a journey worth undertaking. It involves a combination of strategies, including:

1. Developing a Strong Mental Fortress:

Mindfulness and Meditation: Practicing mindfulness helps us become more aware of our thoughts and feelings, enabling us to observe them without judgment. Meditation, on the other hand, teaches us to cultivate a sense of calm and focus, allowing us to manage anxieties more effectively.

Positive Self-Talk: Our thoughts have a powerful influence on our emotions. Engaging in positive self-talk, challenging negative thoughts, and replacing them with affirmations can help shift our mindset from fear to confidence.

Building a Support System: Having a network of supportive friends, family, or mentors can provide encouragement and understanding, offering a safe space to share our anxieties and receive guidance.

2. Embracing Challenges as Growth Opportunities:

Challenging Limiting Beliefs: We all carry limiting beliefs, often based on past experiences or societal conditioning. Identifying these beliefs and challenging them can help us break free from self-imposed limitations and embrace new possibilities.

Focusing on Strengths: Recognizing and highlighting our strengths can boost our self-confidence, enabling us to face challenges with a more positive and empowering mindset.

Learning from Mistakes: Mistakes are inevitable parts of the journey, but they are also valuable learning opportunities. Instead of dwelling on failures, we can embrace them as steppingstones towards growth and success.

3. Taking Measured Steps towards Change:

Setting Realistic Goals: Start small and gradually work towards bigger goals. Breaking down larger tasks into smaller, manageable steps can reduce overwhelm and make the process feel less daunting.

Celebrating Small Victories: Acknowledge and celebrate each step forward, no matter how small it might seem. This helps build momentum and reinforces our belief in our abilities.

Seeking Guidance: Don't be afraid to ask for help or guidance when needed. There are many resources available, from mentors to therapists, to provide support and expertise along the way.

Resilience in the Face of Change

Building resilience isn't a one-time achievement, it's an ongoing process. It requires continuous self-reflection, practice, and a willingness to learn and grow. As we navigate the challenges of life, our resilience will be tested, but it's through these tests that we truly develop our inner strength and ability to face the unknown with courage.

Think of resilience as a muscle that needs to be exercised regularly. The more we practice it, the stronger it becomes, enabling us to handle adversity, embrace change, and achieve our goals.

A Story of Resilience

In the bustling city of Mumbai, amidst the chaos and constant movement, lived a young woman named **Mita**. She had always dreamt of becoming a writer, her heart filled with stories that yearned to be told. But the weight of societal expectations pressed heavily upon her. Her parents, like many others, envisioned a more traditional path, one that led to a stable career in medicine or engineering. They encouraged her to pursue these fields, pushing aside her dreams of becoming a writer, seeing it as an unstable and uncertain career.

The fear of disappointing her parents, of defying their expectations, weighed heavily on Mita. She felt trapped in the confines of their expectations, her own voice silenced by the fear of their disapproval. She enrolled in medical school, fulfilling their dreams, but her heart remained in the world of words.

The fear of change, of stepping outside the comfort of her family's expectations, paralyzed her. The whispers of doubt, the fear of failure, and the anxieties of an uncertain future echoed in her mind. But Mita was not one to let her dreams fade away entirely. She started writing in secret, pouring her heart into stories that reflected her inner world. She joined writing workshops, seeking guidance and support, and her voice, though quiet, began to grow stronger.

Slowly, she started to build her resilience. She practiced mindfulness, focusing on the present moment, calming her anxieties. She challenged her limiting beliefs, reminding herself that she deserved to pursue her passion, that success could be defined on her own terms. She shared her writing with a trusted friend, who offered encouragement and support, reinforcing her belief in her abilities.

One day, Mita finally mustered the courage to share her writing with her parents. She explained her passion, her dreams, and the yearning within her to express herself through words. Her parents, surprised at first, listened intently. They saw the passion in her eyes, the fire of her dreams burning bright.

It wasn't an easy conversation. There were tears, arguments, and a sense of uncertainty. But in the end, Mita's determination and her unwavering belief in herself resonated with her parents. They saw her courage, her resilience, and the strength of her convictions. They agreed to support her dreams, knowing that true happiness lies in pursuing one's passions.

Mita's journey was not without its challenges. She faced rejection, struggled with self-doubt, and navigated the uncertainties of the writing world. But she never gave up. She drew strength from her resilience, from the belief in herself, and from the support of her family. And finally, her story, a testament to her courage and her perseverance, was published, opening the doors to a fulfilling life filled with purpose and passion.

Empowering Your Own Resilience

Mita's story is a testament to the power of resilience, a reminder that change is possible, that we can break free from the confines of fear and limitations, and that we can build a life that reflects our true selves.

Like Mita a, we all have the potential to cultivate resilience, to build our own mental fortresses, and to face the challenges of change with courage. It's a journey that starts with self-awareness, with understanding our fears, and with a commitment to challenge our limiting beliefs. It's a journey that requires practice, patience, and a willingness to step outside our comfort zones, knowing that with each step, we grow stronger, more confident, and more empowered to live a life of purpose and authenticity.

<u>Taking Calculated Risk:</u>

The concept of risk often evokes a sense of fear, a knot tightening in the stomach as we contemplate the potential for loss. Yet, in the grand scheme of personal growth and transformation, calculated risks are not just optional, but essential. They are the steppingstones that lead us out of the familiar and into the unknown, often revealing paths we never imagined.

Think of a seasoned mountain climber. They wouldn't attempt to conquer Everest without meticulously planning their route, assessing weather conditions, and ensuring they have the necessary equipment and expertise. It's the same with taking risks in life. We must approach them with careful consideration, understanding the potential rewards and the possible consequences.

A key step in navigating calculated risks is evaluating the potential outcome. What could you gain if the risk pays off? What would be the worst-case scenario if it doesn't? This exercise forces us to confront our fears and detach from the emotional whirlwind that often accompanies risk-taking. It allows us to analyze the situation objectively, using logic and reason rather than letting fear dictate our choices.

Take the example of a young entrepreneur who dreams of starting their own business. The risk of failure looms large, but so does the potential reward of financial independence and creative fulfillment. By meticulously crafting a business plan, conducting market research, and seeking guidance from experienced mentors, they can mitigate the risks and increase their chances of success.

Remember, calculated risks are not about blind leaps of faith. They are about making informed decisions, carefully weighing the odds, and taking calculated steps towards your goals. It's about understanding that every risk carries a potential reward, and that sometimes, the greatest rewards lie on the other side of fear.

Let's explore a few strategies for evaluating and taking calculated risks:

1. Define Your Goals: Before embarking on any risky venture, it's crucial to have a clear understanding of your goals. What are you hoping to achieve by taking this risk? What is your desired outcome? Having well-defined goals provides a compass for your journey, keeping you focused and motivated even when faced with challenges.

Consider the story of a young woman who dreams of becoming a writer. She has been nurturing this dream for years, but the fear of rejection and failure has kept her from pursuing it. However, one day, she decides to take a calculated risk. She defines her goal – to complete a novel and submit it to publishers. With this goal in mind, she sets aside time each day to write, joins a writing group for feedback, and attends workshops to improve her craft. While the path may be challenging, her clear goal gives her the motivation to overcome her fears and pursue her passion.

2. Assess Your Resources: Every risk requires resources – time, energy, financial support, and perhaps even social connections. Before taking a leap, it's vital to evaluate your available resources and plan accordingly.

A middle-aged man who wants to change careers might have to juggle his current job while taking courses or gaining experience in his new field. This requires careful planning and management of time and resources. He might need to reduce his expenses, negotiate flexible work hours, or seek support from his family. By assessing his resources and planning accordingly, he can mitigate the risks and increase his chances of success in his career transition.

3. Seek Mentorship and Support: Navigating unfamiliar territory is often easier with guidance. Seek mentors who have experience in the area you're considering, whether it's a new career path, a business venture, or a personal change. Their insights, wisdom, and support can provide valuable perspectives and help you avoid common pitfalls.

Consider a young woman who wants to start a social enterprise. She seeks out experienced entrepreneurs and social workers who can mentor her, providing insights into the challenges and rewards of running such an organization. These mentors help her develop a solid business plan, connect her with potential investors, and offer valuable guidance as she navigates the complexities of social entrepreneurship.

4. Start Small: Don't feel the need to take monumental risks all at once. Start with small, manageable steps. This helps you build confidence, gain experience, and assess your commitment before diving in headfirst.

A man who is afraid of public speaking could begin by joining a toastmaster's club, where he can gradually build his confidence by speaking in front of a small group. He can then progress to giving presentations in his workplace or volunteering to speak at community events. This gradual approach helps him build his skills and overcome his fear without feeling overwhelmed.

5. Embrace Flexibility: Things don't always go according to plan. Be prepared to adapt and adjust your approach based on the circumstances. This flexibility can help you navigate unforeseen challenges and keep moving towards your goals.

A young entrepreneur who launched a new product might realize it's not resonating with the target market. Instead of stubbornly persisting with the original plan, she adapts by gathering customer feedback and making necessary adjustments to the product or marketing strategy. This flexibility allows her to learn from her initial mistakes and ultimately achieve greater success.

6. Celebrate Your Wins: No matter how small, each step you take towards your goal is a victory worth celebrating. Acknowledging your achievements, no matter how minor, keeps you motivated and encourages you to keep pushing forward.

A young woman who is trying to break free from a restrictive social circle might start by attending a new event, meeting new people, and challenging her comfort zone. This small step, while seemingly insignificant, is a victory that deserves recognition. It signals her progress towards living a more authentic life and inspires her to take further steps.

7. Learn From Your Mistakes: Mistakes are inevitable, and they are valuable learning opportunities. Embrace them, analyze them, and use them as steppingstones for growth. Don't let setbacks derail your journey; view them as opportunities for improvement.

A young man who failed to get a promotion might feel discouraged. However, instead of dwelling on the disappointment, he analyzes the situation, seeks feedback from his superiors, and identifies areas where he can improve. This self-reflection allows him to learn from his mistakes and become a more effective employee, ultimately increasing his chances of success in the future.

Remember, taking calculated risks is not about seeking adventure or seeking to prove your bravery. It's about growth, self-discovery, and embracing the infinite possibilities that life offers. It's about pushing beyond your self-imposed limitations and creating a life that reflects your truest aspirations. So, take a deep breath, evaluate your goals, and take that first step towards the unknown. The journey may be challenging, but the rewards of calculated risk-taking are often far greater than the comforts of staying within your familiar boundaries.

Creating a Support System:

The journey of change is rarely a solo endeavor. Just as a lone traveler might find themselves lost and vulnerable in unfamiliar territory, so too can individuals embarking on a path of transformation feel overwhelmed and uncertain. This is where the concept of support systems comes into play.

Imagine a young woman named **Usha**, working as a software engineer in Mumbai. She dreams of becoming a writer, but the pressure of her stable career and her parents' expectations keeps her tethered to her current path. Fear of failure and the perceived disapproval of her family keep her from pursuing her passion. However, one day, she confides in a close friend, **Rita**, who is a writer herself. Rita's encouragement, her belief in Usha's talent, and her willingness to offer guidance become a lifeline for Usha. With Rita as a constant source of support, Usha starts to take small steps towards her dream, attending writing workshops, joining online writing communities, and even starting a blog.

Usha's experience highlights the crucial role of support systems in enabling individuals to embrace change. A strong support system can provide emotional fortitude, practical assistance, and unbiased feedback needed to navigate the challenges of transformation. Here's how to build a support system that can empower you on your journey of growth:

> **Identify Your Circle of Trust:** The first step is to identify those individuals who can offer you genuine support. This could include close friends, family members, mentors, or even therapists. Seek out people who possess empathy, understanding, and a willingness to listen without judgment.

> **Communicate Your Goals:** Share your aspirations and anxieties openly with your chosen support system. Communicating your

goals clearly allows your support network to provide tailored encouragement, practical advice, and even accountability mechanisms.

Seek Out Like-Minded Individuals: Joining communities or groups focused on personal growth, change, or specific interests can be incredibly valuable. Connecting with individuals who are also on journeys of transformation can foster a sense of shared understanding and provide a platform for mutual support and inspiration.

Nurture Reciprocal Relationships: A healthy support system involves reciprocity. Just as you receive support, be willing to offer it in return to those within your network. Sharing your own experiences, offering guidance, and celebrating each other's milestones strengthens the bonds and fosters a sense of mutual empowerment.

Leverage Professional Support: In some cases, seeking professional support from therapists, counselors, or life coaches can be incredibly beneficial. These professionals can offer expert guidance, tools, and resources to navigate the complexities of change and address underlying emotional challenges.

Recognize Boundaries: It is important to remember that even within a supportive network, boundaries are essential. Be mindful of your own emotional well-being and avoid allowing others to make choices for you. Set clear expectations about the role your support system plays, while also recognizing the need for personal agency in your journey.

As you navigate the challenges of change, remember that you are not alone. Surrounding yourself with a supportive network of trusted individuals can provide emotional resilience, practical assistance, and unwavering belief you need to confidently embrace a brighter future.

Remember, the journey of change is often a winding and uncertain path, but with the support of those who believe in you, you can navigate the terrain with greater strength and courage.

5

EMBRACING DIVERSITY OF PERSPECTIVES

<u>The Value of Diverse Views:</u>

The world, like a vast tapestry, is woven with threads of diverse experiences, beliefs, and perspectives. Each individual, like a unique strand, brings their own color and texture to the grand design. We are all products of our upbringing, our environment, our experiences, and our encounters with the world around us. This intricate interplay of factors shapes our worldview, our values, and our understanding of the world.

In the bustling tapestry of Indian society, we encounter a kaleidoscope of beliefs, traditions, and ways of life. From the vibrant streets of Mumbai to the serene landscapes of the Himalayas, each corner of India presents a unique lens through which to view the world. This inherent diversity is a source of immense richness and strength. Yet, it's often this diversity that we try to box into neatly defined categories, often losing sight of the nuances and complexities that lie beneath the surface.

Imagine a bustling marketplace, where the scent of spices mingles with the sounds of haggling merchants and the hum of conversations in different languages. A young woman, raised in a traditional family, finds herself drawn to the vibrant colors and textures of the marketplace. She is captivated by the stories woven into the fabrics, the delicate embroidery, and the craftsmanship behind each piece. She begins to see the world through the eyes of the artisans, understanding the dedication, passion, and skill that go into their work. This encounter expands her horizons, challenging her preconceived notions and revealing the richness and beauty that lie beyond her own familiar bubble.

Embracing diversity, in essence, is about acknowledging this richness and complexity. It's about recognizing that there are multiple ways of seeing the world, multiple interpretations of experiences, and multiple approaches to life. It's about stepping out of our comfort zones and entering the unfamiliar, acknowledging the value of different perspectives and welcoming the opportunity to learn and grow.

The benefits of embracing diverse perspectives are multifaceted and far-reaching. They empower us to:

1. See Beyond Our Own Limited View: Our own perspectives, shaped by our personal experiences and biases, can sometimes limit our ability to fully understand the world around us. By engaging with diverse views, we challenge our assumptions, broaden our understanding, and gain a more holistic and nuanced perspective.

2. Foster Empathy and Understanding: When we engage with perspectives different from our own, we begin to see the world through the eyes of others. We gain a deeper understanding of their experiences, their struggles, and their motivations. This empathy allows us to connect with others on a deeper level, fostering understanding, compassion, and stronger relationships.

3. Cultivate Critical Thinking Skills: Engaging with diverse perspectives forces us to critically examine our own beliefs and assumptions. It prompts us to question our own biases, challenge our own convictions, and engage in meaningful discourse. This critical thinking process strengthens our ability to analyze information objectively, make informed decisions, and navigate complex situations.

4. Spark Innovation and Creativity: When we are exposed to diverse perspectives, we encounter new ideas, new ways of thinking, and new approaches to problem-solving. This can lead to breakthroughs, inventions, and innovative solutions that would not have been possible within the confines of our own narrow worldview.

5. Build Stronger Communities: By embracing diversity, we foster a sense of inclusion and belonging within our communities. We create spaces where everyone feels valued, respected, and heard, allowing for open dialogue, collaboration, and mutual growth.

The journey of embracing diversity is not always easy. It requires an openness to challenge our own beliefs, and willingness to listen and learn, and a commitment to fostering understanding. It's about letting go of preconceived notions and embracing the richness and complexity of human experience.

The world is a symphony of voices, each with its own unique melody. Embracing diversity is about listening to this symphony, appreciating the harmony of different notes, and understanding the beauty that lies in the richness of its composition. It's about recognizing that we are all part of a larger tapestry, each strand adding its unique color and texture to the grand design.

As we navigate the complexities of Indian society, let us strive to embrace the diversity of perspectives, to challenge our own limitations, and to foster a culture of understanding and empathy. By embracing the richness of our differences, we create a more vibrant, inclusive, and fulfilling world for ourselves and for generations to come.

Here are some real-life examples of how embracing diverse perspectives can transform lives and communities:

The Story of a Social Entrepreneur: Imagine a young woman from a rural village in India, raised in a conservative environment, who witnesses firsthand the challenges faced by women in her community. Inspired by her own experiences and fueled by a deep sense of empathy, she decides to dedicate her life to empowering women through education and entrepreneurship. She travels to cities, immersing herself in the experiences of urban women, learning about their aspirations, their struggles, and their perspectives. This exposure expands her understanding of women's issues, revealing the diversity of experiences within the female population. With this newfound knowledge, she builds a successful social enterprise that empowers rural women through vocational training and microfinance, creating a positive impact on their lives and communities.

The Power of Interfaith Dialogue: In a diverse nation like India, where people of different faiths live side by side, dialogue and understanding are essential for building harmonious relationships. A group of young individuals from different religious backgrounds decide to create a platform for interfaith dialogue. They organize workshops, seminars, and cultural events, inviting people from various communities to share their experiences, beliefs, and perspectives. Through these interactions, they break down stereotypes, foster empathy, and build bridges of understanding between different faiths. They realize that despite their different beliefs, they share common values of compassion, peace, and justice. These shared values form the foundation for building a stronger, more united community.

The Impact of Inclusive Education: A school in a bustling city embraces a policy of inclusive education, recognizing the importance of accommodating students from diverse backgrounds, abilities, and learning styles. They invest in resources and training for teachers, creating an environment that is welcoming, supportive, and tailored to individual needs. This approach allows students to thrive, regardless of their differences. Students with disabilities feel accepted and empowered, while students from different cultural backgrounds find a space to celebrate their unique identities. The school becomes a vibrant microcosm of Indian society, where diversity is celebrated, and where every student has the opportunity to reach their full potential.

These are just a few examples of the transformative power of embracing diverse perspectives. By fostering empathy, challenging our own biases, and actively engaging with individuals from different backgrounds, we can create a more inclusive, understanding, and fulfilling world. In the tapestry of Indian society, let us weave threads of empathy, compassion, and understanding, creating a masterpiece that celebrates the beauty of our diversity.

Stories of Empathy and Understanding:

Empathy is a powerful force that can bridge divides, foster understanding, and create a more compassionate world. It's about stepping outside our own experiences and seeing the world through another person's eyes, acknowledging their feelings and perspectives, even if we don't fully understand them. In the tapestry of human connection, empathy is the thread that weaves together diverse experiences, creating a rich and vibrant whole.

In India, a land rich in cultural diversity, embracing empathy becomes crucial for navigating the complexities of societal interactions. Each community, each individual, carries a unique story, shaped by their own traditions, beliefs, and lived experiences. Understanding these diverse perspectives can be challenging, especially when confronted with unfamiliar customs or differing opinions. However, it is precisely in these moments of difference that the power of empathy shines brightest.

Let's delve into the stories of individuals who have embraced empathy as a guiding force, transforming their understanding of the world and enriching their own lives:

The Story of Sudha: Sudha, a young woman from a small village in Rajasthan, had always been taught that arranged marriages were the only path to a fulfilling life. Her family, deeply rooted in tradition, believed that finding a partner through arranged marriage ensured stability and happiness. However, Sudha, a bright and independent woman, had dreams beyond the boundaries of her village. She desired a career in medicine, a profession deemed unconventional for women in her community.

When Sudha confessed her aspirations to her family, she was met with resistance. Fear and disapproval hung heavy in the air. They feared that pursuing a career would limit her chances of finding a suitable husband. Sudha found herself at a crossroads, torn between her dreams and the expectations of her loved ones. But then, something unexpected happened. Her grandmother, a wise woman who had always supported Sudha's thirst for knowledge, saw the anguish in her granddaughter's eyes. She had witnessed the changing world, recognizing the value of education and empowerment for women. She decided to stand by Sudha, urging her family to understand her aspirations.

Through compassionate dialogues and empathetic understanding, Sudha's grandmother gently helped her family see the world from Sudha's perspective. They began to understand the strength and determination that fueled her dreams. The village elders, witnessing Sudha's passion and commitment, eventually relented, offering their support.

Sudha's journey exemplifies the power of empathy. It is not about abandoning one's traditions, but about acknowledging the diverse aspirations of individuals within the context of those traditions. Through empathy, Sudha's family was able to see beyond their own preconceived notions, embracing her dreams and paving the way for her to pursue a career that brought her joy and fulfillment.

The Story of Anil: Anil, a young man from a conservative family in Delhi, struggled with his own internal conflict. He was deeply passionate about art, a pursuit considered frivolous and impractical by his family. They urged him to pursue a more "stable" career path, one that would ensure financial security. Anil felt trapped, yearning for creative expression while facing the pressure of societal expectations. He felt isolated, unable to share his true passions with those closest to him.

One day, Anil's older brother, who had always been supportive, invited him for coffee. He listened intently as Anil poured his heart out, sharing his dreams and frustrations. Anil's brother, despite having chosen a traditional career path himself, understood the burning desire for self-expression. He had witnessed Anil's artistic talent firsthand, recognizing the joy it brought him.

Instead of dismissing Anil's aspirations, his brother offered a different perspective. He encouraged Amit to find ways to combine his artistic passion with a stable career, suggesting that perhaps art could be a part of his life, not his entire life. He also reassured Anil that his family, while concerned about his future, ultimately loved and supported him. This empathetic conversation opened a new path for Anil. He began exploring creative careers that combined his artistic talents with financial stability.

Anil's story highlights the power of empathy in creating a space for open dialogue and understanding. It emphasizes the importance of listening not just to words, but to the emotions behind them, and to offer support and encouragement even when our own paths diverge.

The Story of Hema: Hema, a middle-aged woman from Mumbai, worked as a teacher in a school located in a predominantly lower-income neighborhood. She was passionate about her work, deeply invested in the education and well-being of her students. But she often felt frustrated by the societal inequalities that her students faced, inequalities that often hindered their chances of achieving their full potential.

One day, Hema was walking home from school when she encountered a group of children from her class huddling around a street vendor, their faces filled with longing. They were watching a group of children from a wealthier school playing with expensive toys. The scene struck a chord deep within Hema. She understood the children's yearning for a better life, the frustration of being denied opportunities simply because of their socioeconomic background.

That evening, Hema decided to act. She started a small after-school program, using her own time and resources to provide her students with additional educational support and opportunities. She organized fundraising events, rallied her community, and even reached out to other schools, seeking donations of books and learning materials. She sought to create a space where her students could explore their talents, develop their potential, and dream big.

Hema's story demonstrates the profound impact of empathy in addressing societal inequalities. By seeing the world through the eyes of her students, understanding their struggles and aspirations, Maya was able to channel her compassion into action, making a tangible difference in their lives.

These are just a few stories that illustrate the power of empathy in shaping individual lives and creating a more just and compassionate society. Empathy allows us to transcend our own limitations, embracing the richness of human experience. It opens doors to understanding, fostering connections, and building bridges across cultures and perspectives.

The journey of empathy is a lifelong pursuit, requiring constant effort and a willingness to step outside our comfort zones. It is a journey of self-reflection, challenging our own biases, and recognizing the value of diverse perspectives.

As we navigate the complexities of our own lives and the world around us, let us remember that empathy is not a passive emotion but a powerful tool for transformation. It is the key to unlocking our true potential and building a world where every individual feels seen, heard, and valued.

Overcoming Prejudices:

The world is a kaleidoscope of colors, a symphony of sounds, and a tapestry woven with diverse threads. Each thread represents a unique perspective, a distinct way of seeing and experiencing the world. Yet, we often fall prey to the insidious whispers of prejudice, building invisible walls that confine our understanding and limit our connections. These prejudices, rooted in our upbringing, our social circles, and the media we consume, color our perceptions and warp our judgment. Recognizing and overcoming these biases is the first step towards embracing the richness of diverse perspectives.

Prejudices are like hidden lenses through which we view the world. They distort our reality, leading us to make assumptions and generalizations about individuals and groups based on limited information or preconceived notions. We might unconsciously judge someone based on their religion, caste, gender, or skin color, letting stereotypes cloud our ability to see the person behind the label. These biases can manifest in subtle ways, such as unconsciously avoiding eye contact with someone from a different background or making assumptions about someone's intelligence based on their accent.

The journey to overcoming prejudice begins with self-awareness. It requires a willingness to confront our own biases and to honestly examine the thoughts, feelings, and beliefs that shape our judgments. Ask yourself: What assumptions do I make about people based on their appearance or background? How do my beliefs about the world influence my interactions with others? The answers might be uncomfortable, but this introspection is crucial for personal growth and building a more inclusive society.

One effective tool for combatting prejudice is empathy. Imagine stepping into the shoes of someone different from yourself, understanding their experiences, and seeing the world through their lens. Empathy requires active listening, a willingness to suspend judgment, and a genuine desire to connect with others on a deeper level. Engage in conversations with people from diverse backgrounds, listen to their stories, and challenge your own preconceived notions. This process of understanding can be transformative, breaking down the walls of prejudice and opening your mind to new possibilities.

Furthermore, fostering inclusive environments is paramount in dismantling prejudice. Create spaces where people from diverse backgrounds feel comfortable sharing their experiences, perspectives, and ideas. Engage in respectful dialogue, challenge stereotypes, and promote understanding and acceptance. By actively creating inclusive communities, we can create a world where differences are celebrated, and everyone feels a sense of belonging.

Overcoming prejudice is not a one-time event but an ongoing process. It requires constant vigilance, a commitment to continuous learning, and a willingness to challenge our own biases. Embrace the diversity of perspectives, cultivate empathy, and foster inclusive environments. By doing so, we can create a world where everyone feels seen, heard, and valued, and where the richness of human experience can truly flourish.

<u>Learning from Differences:</u>

In a nation as diverse as India, encountering individuals from different backgrounds is a constant reality. From the bustling streets of Mumbai to the serene villages of Kerala, every interaction presents an opportunity to learn from the unique perspectives and experiences of others. This section explores the richness that comes from embracing diversity and learning from individuals with backgrounds unlike our own.

Imagine yourself strolling through a bustling market in Delhi. Amidst the vibrant colors and tantalizing aromas, you strike up a conversation with an elderly vendor, her weathered hands expertly arranging a stack of spices. Her words, laced with the wisdom of generations, paint a vivid picture of a world vastly different from your own. She speaks of ancient traditions, of community bonds that transcend blood ties, of a life lived in harmony with the rhythms of nature. Her story, though vastly different from yours, offers a glimpse into a world of rich cultural heritage, a world where respect for elders, a deep connection to the land, and a strong sense of community are deeply ingrained values.

You might be tempted to simply observe her story as an outsider, taking in the fascinating details without truly engaging. But true learning lies in stepping beyond the comfort of your own perspective and engaging with the other. Ask questions, listen attentively, and allow yourself to be challenged by her viewpoint. Her stories might highlight practices that seem unconventional to you, beliefs that differ from your own. Yet, in those differences lies a wealth of knowledge waiting to be discovered. You might find yourself questioning your own assumptions, challenging your own ingrained biases, and gaining a deeper understanding of the world around you.

Learning from differences isn't solely about acquiring new information; it's about expanding your understanding of humanity itself. It's about recognizing the common thread that binds us together despite our differences, a thread woven from shared emotions, aspirations, and experiences. It's about cultivating empathy, that essential human quality that allows us to connect with others on a deeper level, to step into their shoes and see the world through their eyes.

Take, for instance, the experience of a young woman from a rural village who migrates to a bustling city to pursue higher education. She leaves behind the familiar comfort of her community and the traditions she has always known, stepping into a world of rapid change and unfamiliar expectations. In this new environment, she encounters people from diverse backgrounds, each with their own stories and perspectives. She might find herself surrounded by individuals who are comfortable with expressing their opinions freely, who are driven by individual ambition, and who prioritize personal achievement. Her world, shaped by the values of her village – a strong emphasis on family, a sense of community responsibility, and a slower pace of life – might clash with the values she observes in the city.

This clash of perspectives can be both challenging and enriching. It can spark uncomfortable conversations, challenge her existing beliefs, and push her to confront her own prejudices. But it can also lead to personal growth, a broadening of her understanding of human behavior, and a deeper appreciation for the diversity of human experience. In this new environment, she has the opportunity to learn from the resilience, adaptability, and ambition she observes in her urban peers. She may find herself adopting new perspectives, expanding her own definition of success, and developing a more nuanced view of the world around her.

Learning from differences isn't always about acquiring new information; it's often about unlearning what we believe we know. It's about acknowledging our own biases, those inherent filters that shape our perception of the world. These biases can arise from our upbringing, our cultural background, or even our personal experiences. They can lead us to make snap judgments, to view others through a lens of prejudice, and to limit our understanding of the world around us.

To truly learn from differences, we must first become aware of our own biases. We must be willing to question our assumptions, to challenge our own pre-conceived notions. This requires a conscious effort to step outside of our comfort zones, to engage with perspectives that challenge our own.

For instance, imagine a young man raised in a traditional family, where gender roles are clearly defined and adherence to tradition is highly valued. He may have grown up with a specific set of beliefs about women's roles in society, beliefs that have been passed down through generations. In his world, women are expected to prioritize domestic responsibilities, to support their husbands, and to raise their children. His beliefs, while rooted in his upbringing, might be limiting, preventing him from recognizing the diverse talents and aspirations of women beyond the confines of his own family.

He might encounter a woman who has chosen to pursue a career in STEM, a field traditionally dominated by men. Her story, her struggles, and her achievements could challenge his pre-conceived notions and encourage him to question his own biases. This encounter can spark a conversation about gender roles, about societal expectations, and about the need to redefine what it means to be a successful woman in modern India.

The process of unlearning and relearning is essential for personal growth. It allows us to shed our biases, to embrace new perspectives, and to develop a more compassionate and understanding view of the world.

Learning from differences isn't just about intellectual growth; it's also about fostering a sense of community and belonging. In a diverse society like India, it is crucial to create spaces where individuals from different backgrounds feel welcome, valued, and respected. This requires a conscious effort to build bridges, to foster dialogue, and to celebrate the richness that diversity brings to our lives.

In the realm of business, embracing diversity can be a powerful driver of innovation. When companies foster inclusive environments, they tap into a wider pool of talent, diverse perspectives, and innovative ideas. This can lead to a greater understanding of consumer needs, to the development of products and services that resonate with a broader audience, and ultimately to greater success.

On a personal level, embracing diversity can enrich our lives in countless ways. It can expand our social circles, expose us to new experiences, and create opportunities for personal growth and self-discovery. It can also help us build stronger, more meaningful relationships, grounded in mutual respect, understanding, and empathy.

Learning from differences isn't a passive activity; it requires conscious effort and a willingness to step outside of our comfort zones. It requires us to be open-minded, to be willing to challenge our own beliefs, and to embrace the richness that diversity brings to our lives.

In the tapestry of human existence, diversity is the thread that binds us together. It's a source of strength, resilience, and creativity. By embracing the beauty of our differences, we create a world that is more vibrant, more compassionate, and more fulfilling for all.

<u>Fostering Inclusive Environments:</u>

Fostering inclusive environments is not merely a matter of ticking boxes or adhering to policy guidelines; it's a deeply personal journey of understanding and embracing diversity. It begins with a conscious effort to challenge our own biases and to recognize the inherent worth and dignity of every individual, regardless of their background, beliefs, or experiences.

Imagine a bustling marketplace in a vibrant city. Each stall, each vendor, represents a unique facet of the city's diverse tapestry. Some offer traditional crafts, others showcase modern art, while others specialize in culinary delights from various regions. The beauty lies not only in the variety but also in the harmonious coexistence of these diverse elements. Each stall contributes to the overall richness and vibrancy of the marketplace.

In the same vein, inclusivity in our personal and professional lives thrives when we cultivate an appreciation for the diverse perspectives, talents, and contributions of those around us. We create spaces where individuals feel valued, respected, and empowered to share their unique experiences and insights.

Here's how we can cultivate inclusive environments:

1. Cultivate a Culture of Curiosity and Empathy:

- **Ask open-ended questions:** Instead of making assumptions, engage in genuine conversations that delve into the experiences and perspectives of others. Ask open-ended questions that invite them to share their stories and thoughts.

- **Practice active listening:** When someone is sharing their experiences, truly listen with an open mind and heart. Set aside your own judgments and preconceived notions and strive to understand their point of view.

- **Empathy as a bridge:** Empathy is the key to building bridges across cultural and personal divides. Put yourself in their shoes, attempting to see the world through their lens.

For example, imagine a team meeting where a colleague from a different cultural background is sharing their perspective on a project. Instead of immediately dismissing their ideas or jumping to conclusions, take a moment to genuinely listen and understand their reasoning. Ask clarifying questions to gain a deeper understanding of their cultural context and how it influences their approach.

2. Challenge Implicit Biases and Promote Fair Treatment:

- **Recognize your own biases:** We all hold unconscious biases, shaped by our experiences and social conditioning. The first step is acknowledging their existence and actively seeking to understand their influence on our actions and perceptions.

- **Promote fairness and equality:** Strive to create an environment where everyone has equal opportunities to succeed, regardless of their background or identity. Ensure that policies and procedures are fair and unbiased, and actively combat any form of discrimination or prejudice.

- **Inclusive language matters:** Be mindful of the language we use, ensuring it is inclusive and respectful of everyone. Avoid using language that perpetuates stereotypes or reinforces harmful assumptions.

For instance, in a workplace setting, ensure that performance evaluations are based solely on merit and not influenced by gender, caste, or any other factors irrelevant to job performance. Actively challenge colleagues who make discriminatory comments and promote a culture where such behavior is not tolerated.

3. Create Spaces for Open Dialogue and Authentic Connection:

- **Welcome differences:** Celebrate the unique qualities and backgrounds of each individual, recognizing that diversity enriches our lives and expands our horizons.

- **Encourage open dialogue:** Create safe spaces where people feel comfortable expressing their thoughts and opinions, even if they differ from your own.

- **Promote active engagement:** Encourage everyone to participate in discussions, workshops, and events, fostering a sense of belonging and shared purpose.

For example, organize workshops or events that focus on cultural understanding and appreciation. This can involve inviting speakers from different communities, showcasing diverse perspectives on a particular issue, or engaging in interactive activities that promote dialogue and shared learning.

4. Foster a Culture of Continuous Learning and Growth:

- **Embrace the learning curve:** Acknowledge that fostering inclusive environments is an ongoing process, requiring constant learning, reflection, and adaptation.

- **Seek out diverse perspectives:** Make an effort to expose yourself to different viewpoints, cultures, and experiences. This can involve reading books, watching films, attending workshops, or engaging in conversations with people from diverse backgrounds.

- **Learn from your mistakes:** If you find yourself making an insensitive or discriminatory comment, acknowledge your error and learn from it. Use it as an opportunity to grow and become more conscious of your actions.

For instance, in a professional setting, consider organizing learning sessions or workshops on topics such as cultural sensitivity, implicit bias, and inclusive leadership. These initiatives can empower individuals to become more aware of their biases and develop strategies for promoting inclusion in their daily interactions.

5. Celebrate the Value of Diversity:

- **Acknowledge the richness of diversity:** Recognize that diversity enriches our lives, broadens our perspectives, and fosters creativity.

- **Recognize and celebrate cultural contributions:** Acknowledge and appreciate the unique contributions that individuals from different backgrounds bring to our communities.

- **Highlight success stories:** Share stories of individuals who have overcome adversity or achieved success through embracing diversity.

For example, organize events or activities that showcase the talents and achievements of individuals from diverse backgrounds. This could involve hosting cultural performances, featuring diverse artwork, or highlighting the contributions of individuals from different communities to the workplace or the local area.

In conclusion, fostering inclusive environments is an essential journey that requires constant effort and commitment. It's about recognizing the inherent worth of every individual, embracing diversity as a strength, and actively working to create spaces where everyone feels valued, respected, and empowered. By cultivating a culture of curiosity, empathy, and understanding, we can build bridges across cultural divides and create a world where everyone has the opportunity to thrive.

6

THE LIBERATION OF LETTING GO

<u>Understanding Attachment:</u>

In the tapestry of life, we are all interconnected, threads woven together by invisible forces of attachment. These bonds, though seemingly benign, can often transform into invisible chains, tethering us to the past, holding us back from embracing the present and the promise of a brighter future. This intricate dance between connection and liberation is what we explore in this chapter, delving into the complex world of attachment and its profound impact on our personal journeys.

Attachment is an inherent part of human experience. It is the natural tendency to seek connection, comfort, and security in relationships. From the moment we are born, we are wired to crave the warmth of our parents' embrace, the reassurance of their presence. This deep-seated need for belonging extends beyond our early years, shaping our relationships with friends, lovers, family, and even material possessions.

However, the flip side of this profound need for connection is the potential for attachment to become a source of limitation. When attachment becomes excessive, it can morph into an unhealthy dependence, a fear of losing the familiar, and a resistance to letting go. It can manifest in various ways, from clinging to relationships that are no longer serving us, to holding onto past hurts and resentments, to accumulating material possessions that offer a false sense of security.

Imagine a young woman, **Payal**, raised in a traditional Indian household. From a tender age, she was instilled with the belief that a woman's life was defined by marriage and motherhood. As she grew older, this belief became ingrained, shaping her choices and desires. She pursued a career that would make her parents proud, but secretly, she yearned for something more. Yet, the fear of disappointing her family, the deep-seated attachment to their expectations, kept her chained to a path that felt increasingly suffocating.

Payal's story is a reflection of the many individuals who find themselves caught in the grip of attachment, their choices dictated by the weight of expectations and the fear of venturing beyond the familiar. This type of attachment can be particularly powerful in India, where familial and societal norms play a significant role in shaping individual choices. It can lead to feelings of obligation, guilt, and a constant struggle to live up to external standards.

But attachment is not just limited to relationships with people. We can become deeply attached to material possessions, viewing them as sources of comfort, security, and identity. We might feel a sense of ownership over these items, believing that they define our worth and bring us happiness. This attachment can lead to a cycle of consumerism, a relentless pursuit of the latest gadgets, designer clothes, and luxurious experiences, often leaving us feeling empty and dissatisfied.

Imagine a young man, **Rajat**, who has spent years meticulously crafting his life according to a specific image of success. He holds a high-paying job, drives a fancy car, lives in a luxurious apartment, and surrounds himself with the latest gadgets. He believes that these material possessions are proof of his achievements, a reflection of his worthiness and his place in society. However, beneath the surface of this carefully constructed façade, he feels a growing emptiness, a yearning for something more meaningful. The constant need to accumulate, to acquire more, to keep up with the Joneses, is a symptom of his unhealthy attachment to material possessions.

The liberating power of letting go begins with recognizing the nature of our attachments. It requires honesty and self-awareness, a willingness to examine our beliefs and desires, and to question the stories we tell ourselves about what brings us happiness and fulfillment. As we become aware of the chains of attachment, we can start to loosen their grip.

> Imagine a seasoned businessman, **Amish**, who has dedicated his life to building a successful career, a pursuit that has consumed his time, energy, and attention. He has achieved financial success, but his personal life has been neglected, his relationships strained by his relentless pursuit of material wealth. One day, a health scare forces him to re-evaluate his priorities. He realizes that his life has become a relentless chase, an endless pursuit of something that has failed to bring him true happiness.

Amish's journey of letting go begins with a decision to prioritize his health and well-being. He gradually sheds the burden of workaholism, reclaiming his time and attention. He starts to engage in activities that nourish his soul, spending time with loved ones, rediscovering his passion for music, and embracing a simpler lifestyle. This act of letting go, of releasing the grip of attachment, leads him to a sense of peace, contentment, and true fulfillment that he had never known before.

Letting go is not about detachment from all relationships and possessions. It is about recognizing the difference between healthy and unhealthy attachment. It is about cultivating a sense of freedom, a lightness of being, that comes from being present in the moment, appreciating the beauty of simplicity, and living with intention.

In the ancient Indian philosophy of Advaita Vedanta, the concept of "non-attachment" is central to achieving a state of inner peace and liberation. This philosophy emphasizes the impermanence of all things, encouraging us to detach from the outcomes of our actions and find contentment in the journey itself. By surrendering to the present moment, accepting the ebb and flow of life, and releasing the grip of our desires, we can break free from the shackles of attachment and experience true liberation.

The path to liberation through letting go is not a linear journey. It is a process of self-discovery, a gradual unwinding of the invisible chains that bind us. It requires courage to challenge our deeply ingrained patterns, to step outside of our comfort zones, and to embrace the unknown. It is a journey of letting go of expectations, of shedding limiting beliefs, and of learning to embrace the present moment with a grateful heart.

As we navigate this journey of letting go, we can draw inspiration from the stories of those who have gone before us. We can learn from the wisdom of yogis, saints, and spiritual teachers who have devoted their lives to understanding the nature of attachment and the path to liberation. We can seek support from loved ones, mentors, and therapists who can guide us through the challenges and celebrate our triumphs.

The journey of letting go is a journey of self-discovery, a path that leads us to a deeper understanding of ourselves and our place in the world. It is a journey that requires courage, compassion, and a willingness to embrace the unknown. It is a journey that ultimately leads to freedom, a freedom from the limitations of our attachments, a freedom to live a life of authenticity, purpose, and joy.

In the end, the liberation of letting go is not about losing something but rather about gaining a new perspective, a deeper sense of peace, and a renewed capacity for love, connection, and fulfillment. It is about living a life that is not defined by possessions, relationships, or expectations but by a deep and abiding connection to our true selves, a connection that transcends the boundaries of time and space.

<u>Stories of Release and Freedom:</u>

The stories of release and freedom are as diverse as the individuals who experience them. In the tapestry of human existence, each thread, representing a life, holds a unique narrative of its own. In these stories, we witness the power of letting go - of relinquishing the chains of attachment, expectations, and limiting beliefs that bind us.

Take, for instance, the story of **Mayuri**, a young woman who grew up in a traditional Indian family, burdened by the weight of societal expectations. Her life revolved around finding a suitable husband, getting married, and having children. This was the path laid out for her, the script she was expected to follow. But Mayuri had a different script in her heart, a desire to pursue a career in art, a passion that had been buried under layers of societal pressure.

For years, she suppressed her dreams, her heart heavy with the guilt of defying her family's expectations. But one day, a pivotal moment arrived - a visit to a renowned art exhibition ignited a spark within her. It was a reminder of her forgotten dreams, a whisper of a possibility that resonated with her soul. It was a call to liberation.

Mayuri decided to let go of the pre-written script and embrace the freedom of writing her own story. She enrolled in an art school, defying her family's disapproval. The initial stages were filled with fear and uncertainty. She questioned her decision, her heart trembling at the thought of shattering the expectations that had shaped her life. But she persevered, fueled by a deep-seated desire to live a life true to herself.

The journey wasn't easy. She faced criticism, skepticism, and even alienation from her family. But through it all, Mayuri held onto her dreams, her heart unwavering in its pursuit of freedom. She channeled her emotions into her art, each stroke of the brush a testament to her strength and determination.

With time, her talent blossomed, her art gaining recognition and appreciation. The world began to see her not as a daughter who had defied expectations, but as an artist who had embraced her true calling. Mayuri's story is a powerful testament to liberation that comes from letting go of societal expectations, embracing our own passions, and daring to live life on our own terms.

Another story, that of **Ravi**, a successful businessman, demonstrates the liberating power of letting go of material attachments. Ravi had spent years climbing the corporate ladder, driven by ambition and a relentless pursuit of success. He accumulated wealth, acquired luxurious possessions, and built a seemingly perfect life. But behind the façade of success, a deep sense of emptiness gnawed at his soul.

Ravi realized that his life had become a relentless chase, a quest for external validation that had left him feeling drained and unfulfilled. He felt trapped in a cycle of work and consumption, his spirit yearning for something more meaningful. One day, while reflecting on his life, he stumbled upon a quote by the Dalai Lama: "Happiness is not something readymade. It comes from your own actions."

This simple yet profound message resonated with Ravi. It was a wake-up call, an invitation to re-evaluate his priorities and find happiness in something other than material possessions. He decided to let go of his attachments, to simplify his life and pursue something that truly ignited his spirit.

Ravi sold his luxurious home, donated a significant portion of his wealth to charity, and embarked on a journey of self-discovery. He traveled to remote villages, immersing himself in different cultures, witnessing the resilience and joy of communities who lived simpler lives. He discovered a sense of contentment, a peace that he had never experienced before.

Ravi's story illustrates the power of letting go of material attachments, of finding fulfillment in experiences, relationships, and purpose rather than possessions. It highlights the liberating truth that true happiness lies within, not in the accumulation of things.

These stories, while vastly different, share a common thread - they showcase the liberating power of letting go. They demonstrate that by releasing ourselves from the shackles of expectations, attachments, and limiting beliefs, we unlock the potential for a richer, more fulfilling life.

These are just glimpses into a vast universe of stories, each holding its own unique narrative of liberation. As we delve deeper into the experiences of individuals who have found freedom through letting go, we gain a deeper understanding of the transformative power of embracing change, challenging our own beliefs, and living life on our own terms.

From the confines of our comfort zones to the weight of societal expectations, the shackles of limiting beliefs, and the fear of change, these stories unveil the liberating power of letting go. They showcase individuals who have bravely stepped out of their "brackets," embracing the infinite possibilities that lie beyond the walls of their own perceptions. They inspire us to explore the vast terrain of our own existence, to challenge the narratives that have shaped our lives, and to create a life that is authentic, fulfilling, and true to our own hearts.

The stories of release and freedom are not merely narratives of personal transformation. They are a testament to the inherent human spirit's ability to break free from limitations and embrace the boundless possibilities that life offers. In these stories, we find not just inspiration but also a roadmap to our own liberation, a call to break free from the

confines of our "brackets" and embark on a journey of self-discovery, empathy, and authentic living.

Let these stories be a reminder that the freedom we seek is not outside of us; it is within, waiting to be unleashed. It is in the courage to let go, to embrace change, to redefine success, and to live a life that resonates with our true selves. Let us embark on this journey of liberation, inspired by the stories of those who have gone before us, and empowered by the belief that a life of freedom and fulfillment is within our reach.

<u>Practicing Detachment:</u>

Imagine a bird in a gilded cage. The bars are intricately crafted, the surroundings opulent, yet the bird remains confined. It can see the vast, open sky beyond, but it can't touch it. The bird has everything it needs within the cage, but it can never truly experience the freedom of flight. This is the analogy of our lives when we hold onto attachments – we may have everything we desire, but we remain tethered, unable to experience the true depth of joy and liberation.

In the tapestry of life, detachment plays a crucial role in unlocking a profound sense of freedom. It is not about indifference or apathy; it's about understanding that our happiness isn't bound to external circumstances or possessions. Detachment allows us to appreciate the present moment without clinging to outcomes or fearing loss. It is about finding joy in the journey, not just the destination.

> Imagine a young woman named **Navya**, a budding entrepreneur in Mumbai. She poured her heart and soul into building her business, dedicating countless hours to its success. She thrived on the validation that came with each milestone achieved, each client gained. Navya was deeply attached to her business, believing its success was directly tied to her own happiness. When a sudden economic downturn struck, impacting her business significantly, Navya felt shattered. Her world seemed to crumble, and her sense of self was deeply affected.

Navya's story reflects a common trap: clinging to external validation and material possessions. When these external factors are disrupted, we feel a profound sense of loss and emptiness. However, detachment allows us to navigate life's ups and downs with greater resilience. It allows us to find contentment even when external circumstances are challenging, knowing that our true happiness doesn't hinge on external achievements or possessions.

Practicing Detachment: A Journey of Liberation

Detachment is not a state of passive resignation; it's an active choice we make to loosen our grip on things that hold us back. It's a gradual process, requiring conscious effort and self-reflection. It's about cultivating a sense of acceptance and letting go of the need to control everything around us.

Here are some techniques to cultivate a healthy sense of detachment:

1. Mindful Observation: Start by observing your thoughts and feelings without judgment. When you experience a wave of attachment, notice it without labeling it as good or bad. Observe the emotions, sensations, and impulses associated with it. This awareness allows you to gain a more objective perspective on your thoughts and emotions.

For instance, if you find yourself constantly worrying about the outcome of a presentation, gently acknowledge this thought without letting it consume you. You can say to yourself, "I'm noticing this worry about the presentation. I'm allowing myself to feel it without judgment." This simple act of observation creates a space between you and your thoughts, allowing you to gain some distance from them.

2. Cultivating Gratitude: Focusing on the positive aspects of your life shifts your attention away from what you lack and towards what you have. Expressing gratitude for even the simplest things, like a cup of tea or a beautiful sunset, helps to cultivate a sense of contentment and appreciation for the present moment.

Think about a day in your life. What are the things you're grateful for?

Perhaps it's the warmth of the sun on your skin, a delicious meal, or a supportive friend. Making a conscious effort to appreciate these small moments creates a sense of abundance and reduces the need to grasp onto things that can be easily lost.

3. Acceptance and Letting Go: Embrace the impermanence of life. Accept that nothing is permanent and learn to let go of things that are no longer serving you. This includes material possessions, relationships that no longer bring joy, and beliefs that no longer resonate with your current self.

Imagine holding a pebble in your hand. If you hold it too tightly, it can create discomfort and even pain. But if you loosen your grip, the pebble can rest comfortably in your palm. Similarly, holding onto things too tightly in life can cause stress and anxiety. Letting go of these attachments allows for greater peace and freedom.

4. Cultivating Mindfulness: Mindfulness is the practice of focusing on the present moment without judgment. Engaging in mindfulness exercises like meditation or mindful breathing helps to quiet the mind, reduce stress, and cultivate a sense of inner peace.

When you practice mindfulness, you bring your attention to the present moment, noticing sensations in your body, sounds around you, and the rhythm of your breath. This allows you to become more aware of your thoughts and feelings without getting swept away by them.

5. Finding Purpose Beyond Possessions: Shift your focus from material possessions to finding purpose and meaning in your life. Engage in activities that bring you joy and contribute to something greater than yourself.

Think about your values and what truly matters to you. What brings you a sense of fulfillment? It could be spending time with loved ones, pursuing your passions, or making a positive impact on the world. Aligning your actions with your values creates a deeper sense of purpose and satisfaction that transcends external achievements or possessions.

6. Setting Boundaries: Setting healthy boundaries is crucial for detachment. It allows you to protect your time, energy, and well-being. This means learning to say no to requests or commitments that drain you, and prioritizing activities that align with your values.

Imagine you're surrounded by a circle. Inside the circle are the things you prioritize: your well-being, your goals, your loved ones. Outside the circle there are things that can potentially drain your energy or distract you from your priorities. Setting boundaries means learning to say "no" to requests or commitments that fall outside your circle, even if they seem appealing.

7. Engaging in Self-Reflection: Make time for introspection and self-reflection. Journaling, meditation, or simply taking a quiet walk can provide valuable opportunities to explore your thoughts and emotions. Examine your attachments, identify patterns, and reflect on how they impact your overall well-being.

Think of self-reflection as a mirror. It helps you see yourself more clearly, revealing your thoughts, feelings, and behaviors. By reflecting on your experiences, you gain a deeper understanding of yourself and your attachments.

The Journey of Letting Go: Stories of Liberation

The path to detachment is not always easy, but it's a journey worth taking. Here are some stories that illustrate the power of letting go:

The Story of the Elderly Couple: In the bustling city of Delhi, lived an elderly couple, **Hari** and **Pooja**. They had spent their lives accumulating possessions – a large house, an impressive collection of antiques, and a wardrobe overflowing with clothes. However, as they aged, they found themselves increasingly burdened by the weight of their possessions. Their home felt like a museum rather than a haven.

One day, a young volunteer at a local NGO approached them, sharing stories of children in need. Hari and Pooja, touched by the stories, decided to donate a significant portion of their belongings to the NGO. Initially, they felt a twinge of sadness letting go of things they had held for so long. But as they saw the joy on the faces of the children receiving their donations, a new sense of lightness filled their hearts. They realized that true happiness wasn't about material possessions but about contributing to something bigger than themselves.

The Story of the Workaholic: In the corporate world of Mumbai, **Ronit** was known as the "workaholic." He dedicated himself to his career, often sacrificing personal time and relationships. He believed that his success was solely defined by his achievements at work. However, the constant pressure and the relentless pursuit of recognition took a toll on his well-being. He felt drained and unfulfilled despite his professional accomplishments.

One evening, while walking home, Ronit noticed a group of children playing cricket in a park. He stopped to watch, their carefree laughter reminding him of a simpler time. A wave of longing washed over him – he missed the joy of connecting with people on a deeper level. Ronit realized that he had been so focused on climbing the corporate ladder that he had neglected his personal life. He decided to make a change, setting healthier boundaries and prioritizing time for family and friends. He discovered that his true purpose lay in building meaningful connections, not just chasing professional success.

The Story of the Hoarder: In the quiet town of Mysore, resided an elderly woman named **Padma**. She had a deep attachment to objects, finding comfort in their presence. Her home was filled with items from her past, each holding a memory. But as the years passed, her home became cluttered, and her life felt suffocated by the sheer volume of her possessions.

One day, Padma's niece, a young therapist, visited her and noticed the strain on her aunt's face. She suggested Padma consider decluttering her home, starting with the items that no longer served her. Padma felt a wave of resistance initially, but her niece gently encouraged her, emphasizing the importance of letting go of things that weighed her down. Slowly, Padma began to release her attachments, donating items to charity and discarding those that had lost their meaning. The process was challenging, but each item she let go of brought a sense of lightness and liberation. She realized that true happiness didn't lie in clinging to the past but in embracing the present.

These stories illustrate the liberating power of detachment. It allows us to shed the weight of past experiences and embrace the present moment, living with a lighter heart and a more open mind. Detachment doesn't mean we become indifferent to the world around us. It means we cultivate a more balanced perspective, embracing both the joys and challenges of life with grace and resilience.

The Fruits of Detachment: Living a Fulfilling Life

As we practice detachment, we begin to experience a profound shift in our perspective and our relationship with ourselves and the world around us. Here are some of the benefits we can expect:

Increased Happiness and Contentment: When we are not bound by attachments, we become less susceptible to external influences that can disrupt our inner peace. We find joy in the simple pleasures of life and appreciate the present moment without clinging to outcomes.

Greater Resilience: Life is full of ups and downs. When we are not overly attached to things, we can navigate challenges with greater ease, knowing that our happiness is not dependent on external factors. We are less likely to be consumed by fear, anger, or despair when things don't go our way.

Improved Relationships: Detachment allows us to build more authentic and fulfilling relationships. We are less likely to cling to people or demand they meet our expectations, allowing for a more genuine connection.

Clarity and Purpose: When we let go of distractions and attachments, we create space for clarity and self-discovery. We can identify our true values and priorities, leading us towards a more purposeful and fulfilling life.

Inner Peace: Cultivating detachment leads to a profound sense of inner peace. We become less reactive to external stimuli and experience a sense of tranquility even amidst life's chaos.

The journey of detachment is a lifelong practice, an ongoing process of letting go and embracing the present moment. It requires patience, self-awareness, and a willingness to embrace the beauty of imperfection. It is a journey of liberation, a path towards living a more fulfilling and authentic life.

Remember, it's not about becoming a hermit, devoid of all attachments. It's about cultivating a balanced perspective, recognizing that true happiness comes from within, and letting go of the need to control everything around us. The fruits of detachment are truly enriching, leading to a life filled with joy, purpose, and inner peace.

<u>Finding Joy in Simplicity:</u>

The liberation of letting go isn't about abandoning everything you hold dear; it's about recognizing that true joy often lies in shedding unnecessary burdens. We live in a world that relentlessly pushes us to accumulate – possessions, achievements, even relationships. We are constantly bombarded with messages that equate happiness with "more." But what if happiness doesn't reside in the quantity of what we own, but in the quality of what we hold dear?

Think of a tree laden with fruit. The weight of the fruit can be overwhelming, causing branches to bend and even break. Letting go of some of the fruit, while it might seem counterintuitive, allows the tree to thrive. It allows the remaining fruit to ripen, ensuring a richer harvest. This principle applies to our lives as well. By releasing the unnecessary weight of attachment, we free ourselves to experience a greater joy, a deeper sense of peace, and a more vibrant connection with the world around us.

Imagine a woman named **Jaya**, who spent her life accumulating things. From her youth, she had been taught that material possessions were a sign of success. She toiled relentlessly, collecting designer handbags, exotic vacations, and a sprawling house. But even as she achieved these outward markers of success, Jaya found herself feeling strangely empty. She felt suffocated by the weight of her possessions. The house she had poured her heart and soul into building was now a source of anxiety, demanding constant upkeep and maintenance. The beautiful things she had accumulated were now mere objects, devoid of meaning or joy.

One day, Jaya stumbled upon a small, unassuming book titled "The Simplicity of Letting Go." As she read the words, a profound shift began to occur within her. She started to understand that true joy wasn't found in owning more, but in experiencing more. She started to declutter her life, letting go of possessions that no longer served her. She sold her sprawling mansion and moved into a modest apartment, freeing herself from the burden of upkeep. She discovered that she was far more content with less. Instead of spending her weekends cleaning and maintaining her possessions, she started spending more time exploring nature, pursuing hobbies, and connecting with loved ones.

Jaya's journey towards simplicity wasn't a radical shift; it was a gradual process of shedding unnecessary baggage. Each decision to let go was a small act of liberation, a step toward rediscovering the joy that had been buried under the weight of her possessions. She began to find contentment in the simple pleasures – a cup of tea on a sunny morning, the laughter of children, the quiet beauty of a blooming flower.

The act of letting go isn't about denying yourself experiences or pleasures; it's about making conscious choices about what truly brings you joy. It's about prioritizing experiences over possessions, relationships over material wealth, and moments of connection over material accumulation.

We often cling to things out of fear – fear of loss, fear of scarcity, fear of missing out. But the truth is, holding onto things that no longer serve us only creates a sense of stagnation and limitation. By letting go of the need to control and possess, we free ourselves from the shackles of fear. We open ourselves to the possibility of new experiences, new connections, and new sources of joy.

Imagine a young man named **Param**, who was constantly striving for perfection. He felt pressured to excel in every aspect of his life, from his career to his relationships. He poured his energy into attaining external validation, working tirelessly to achieve accolades and recognition. But the harder he pushed, the emptier he felt. He was living in a state of constant striving, never truly satisfied.

One day, while meditating, Param realized the source of his dissatisfaction. He was holding onto the illusion of control, striving to achieve an unrealistic ideal of perfection. He understood that true joy wouldn't come from external validation, but from accepting himself, flaws and all. He began to practice self-compassion, forgiving himself for past mistakes and recognizing that he didn't need to be perfect to be worthy of love and happiness. He started to let go of the need to control every aspect of his life, accepting that some things are simply beyond his control.

Param's journey towards letting go was a journey of self-discovery. He learned that true liberation comes from accepting our imperfections, embracing our vulnerabilities, and releasing the need to control everything. It's about trusting the flow of life, knowing that we are enough, exactly as we are.

Letting go isn't about abandoning our dreams or ambitions; it's about pursuing them with a lighter heart, without the weight of unnecessary attachments. It's about embracing the journey, knowing that life is not about reaching a destination, but about savoring the journey itself.

Think of a bird that has flown for thousands of miles, finally reaching its destination. It has a choice – it can hold onto its weary wings, clinging to the satisfaction of its journey, or it can release the weight of its flight and soar into the next adventure. Letting go isn't about denying the past; it's about appreciating the past and embracing the present with a lightness of being.

The path to liberation through letting go is a journey of self-discovery, a process of stripping away layers of unnecessary baggage and rediscovering the essential joy that lies within. It's about recognizing that true joy isn't found in accumulating more, but in experiencing more, in connecting more deeply with ourselves and the world around us.

This journey begins with a simple act of awareness. Pay attention to the things you cling to – possessions, relationships, ideas, even emotions. Ask yourself: What is this attachment serving? Is it bringing me joy or is it creating a sense of restriction and limitation? Is this something that is truly essential to my well-being, or is it something I can let go of?

The answers may not be easy, but with practice and a willingness to explore, you can start to shed the weight of unnecessary attachments. As you let go, you will discover a new lightness of being, a renewed sense of freedom, and a deeper connection with the true essence of your being.

The practice of letting go is a journey, not a destination. It's a continual process of shedding old patterns and embracing new possibilities. It's about finding joy in the simplicity of being present, in the beauty of the moment, in the richness of human connection, and in the infinite possibilities that life offers.

This journey of letting go is not about denying ourselves the joys of life, but about appreciating them with a lighter heart, a heart that is free from the shackles of unnecessary attachments. It's about embracing the freedom that comes from recognizing that true joy is not found in what we own, but in who we are, in how we choose to live, and in the way we connect with the world around us.

There are many practices that can aid in letting go, such as meditation, mindfulness, journaling, and spending time in nature. Each of these practices helps us to become more aware of our thoughts, emotions, and attachments. They allow us to step back from our automatic reactions and make conscious choices about what we hold onto and what we let go of.

For example, **Mindfulness** teaches us to pay attention to the present moment without judgment. By focusing on our senses, we can develop a greater appreciation for the simple things in life – the warmth of the sun on our skin, the sound of birds singing, the taste of fresh fruit. This practice helps us to detach from our worries and anxieties, allowing us to experience a sense of peace and contentment.

Meditation, on the other hand, helps us to quiet the mind and connect with our inner selves. Through regular practice, we can learn to observe our thoughts and emotions without identifying with them. This practice helps us to break free from the grip of our ego, allowing us to experience a greater sense of freedom and liberation.

Journaling is another helpful tool for letting go. By writing down our thoughts and feelings, we can gain a better understanding of ourselves and our attachments. Journaling can also help us to identify and release negative patterns of thought and behavior.

Spending time in nature can also be a powerful way to let go. The natural world has a way of reminding us of the beauty and simplicity of life. By spending time in nature, we can reconnect with our senses, find peace and quiet, and release the weight of our worries and anxieties.

Ultimately, the journey of letting go is a personal one. There is no one right way to do it. What matters most is finding practices that resonate with you and help you to develop a greater sense of awareness, peace, and freedom.

By embracing the practice of letting go, we can create a life that is more fulfilling, more meaningful, and more joyful. We can free ourselves from the weight of unnecessary attachments and discover the true essence of our being. We can experience the liberation that comes from living with a lighter heart, a heart that is open to the beauty and possibilities of life.

<u>Building a Life of Purpose:</u>

The journey of letting go is not about becoming indifferent or cold. It's about finding freedom from the chains of attachment that hold us back from experiencing life in its fullness. It's about shifting our focus from accumulating possessions and chasing external validation to embracing the richness of our inner world.

Imagine a vast, shimmering lake. It's a beautiful sight, with sunlight reflecting off its surface, creating a tapestry of light and color. But beneath the surface, hidden from view, are layers of sediment. These sediments represent the attachments we carry to material things, to societal expectations, to our own ego and its desires.

As we live, we accumulate these sediments. They weigh us down, making it harder to move freely, to experience the true depth and clarity of life. The practice of letting go is about clearing these sediments, about allowing ourselves to be open to the flow of life without the baggage of attachment.

Finding Meaning in Purpose

Letting go of material possessions and external validation doesn't mean we should become hermits or abandon the pursuit of success. It means redefining success. It means shifting our focus from what we own to what we contribute, from what we achieve to the impact we make.

This is the essence of living a life of purpose. When we align our actions with something greater than ourselves, we tap into a wellspring of meaning and fulfillment that no amount of material wealth or external recognition can provide.

The Pursuit of Purpose

Finding purpose is a journey of self-discovery. It involves exploring our passions, our values, and our skills. It's about asking ourselves:

What truly excites me? What activities do I lose myself in, where time seems to disappear?

What are my core values? What principles do I hold dear and want to live by?

What unique skills and talents do I possess? How can I use these to make a positive difference in the world?

The answers to these questions will lead us down a path of purposeful living. It might be starting a small business that aligns with our passion for social justice, volunteering our time to a cause we believe in, or pursuing a creative outlet that brings us joy and fulfillment.

The Power of Contribution

Imagine a tree. Its roots dig deep into the earth, drawing nourishment and stability. But it also reaches towards the sun, spreading its branches and leaves. In the same way, we need to nurture our inner selves, but also reach out and make a contribution to the world around us.

When we give of ourselves, whether through acts of service, creative expression, or simply showing kindness to others, we experience a sense of interconnectedness and belonging. We become part of something larger than ourselves, and we find meaning in the act of giving.

The Benefits of Purposeful Living

Living a life of purpose has profound benefits:

Increased Well-being: A sense of purpose is a powerful antidote to stress and anxiety. It gives us direction and meaning, allowing us to navigate life's challenges with greater resilience.

Enhanced Relationships: When we live a life aligned with our values, our relationships become more authentic and fulfilling. We attract people who resonate with our purpose and contribute to our growth.

Greater Fulfillment: Purposeful living is not about achieving a specific goal or reaching a certain level of success. It's about living a life that is meaningful to us, where our actions are aligned with our values and our contribution makes a positive impact.

The Journey Begins Within

The journey of letting go and finding purpose is not about seeking external validation or accumulating material possessions. It's about delving into the depths of our own beings, discovering our authentic selves, and aligning our lives with what truly matters. It's about embracing the richness of the present moment, cherishing our connections with others, and leaving a positive mark on the world.

Like a river that carves its way through the landscape, our purpose is constantly evolving. It's not a destination, but a journey of growth and discovery. It's about embracing the unknown, adapting to change, and remaining open to the unfolding of life's experiences.

Simple Practices for Cultivating Purpose

Here are some simple practices you can incorporate into your daily life to cultivate a life of purpose:

Journaling: Take some time each day to reflect on your values, your passions, and your aspirations. Journaling can help you to clarify your purpose and track your progress on your journey.

Mindfulness: Practice mindfulness exercises, such as meditation, to connect with your inner self and cultivate a sense of gratitude for the present moment.

Acts of Service: Find ways to give back to your community, whether through volunteering, donating to a cause you care about, or simply offering a helping hand to someone in need.

Creative Expression: Explore creative outlets such as writing, painting, music, or dance to express your unique talents and perspectives.

Nature Connection: Spend time in nature, allowing yourself to be inspired by its beauty and wisdom.

Remember, the journey of finding purpose is a deeply personal one. It's a path of self-discovery, exploration, and constant growth. Be patient with yourself, trust your intuition, and embrace the adventure that awaits.

7

THE ADVANTAGE OF SELF-DISCOVERY

<u>The Journey Inward:</u>

The journey inward is a profound and often challenging voyage of self-discovery. It's a quest to delve into the depths of our own being, to understand the motivations, beliefs, and experiences that shape who we are. This journey isn't about seeking perfection; it's about embracing the entirety of our selves – the complexities, contradictions, and vulnerabilities that make us human.

Imagine a vast ocean, its surface shimmering under the sun, a serene facade that hides the churning depths beneath. This is often how we present ourselves to the world – a polished exterior masking the intricate currents of our thoughts and emotions. The journey inward is like diving into that ocean, leaving behind the familiar surface and descending into the unknown. It's about facing the anxieties, fears, and doubts that we may have buried deep within, allowing ourselves to see them for what they are, and ultimately, to understand them.

This journey is not always comfortable. It may involve confronting painful memories, confronting ingrained beliefs, or questioning our own assumptions about the world and ourselves. But the rewards are immeasurable. Through self-discovery, we gain a deeper understanding of our own strengths and weaknesses, our values, and our aspirations. We learn to navigate our emotions with greater clarity, to make choices aligned with our true selves, and to build more authentic and fulfilling relationships.

There are many paths that lead to this inward journey. Some may find solace in solitude, in the quiet contemplation of nature or the depths of their own thoughts. Others may find it in the crucible of challenging relationships, where they learn to navigate complex dynamics and understand their own emotional responses. For some, the journey may unfold through creative pursuits – painting, writing, music – where they express the nuances of their inner world through artistic expression.

The key is to be receptive, to allow ourselves to be present in the moment and to truly listen to the whispers of our own hearts. This isn't about finding quick fixes or seeking to change who we are; it's about accepting ourselves fully, flaws and all.

Let's look at a few examples of how this journey unfolds in the lives of ordinary people:

A young woman named **Ruhi**, a software engineer in Bangalore, found herself caught in a vicious cycle of self-doubt and comparison. She excelled in her field, yet felt an underlying sense of inadequacy, constantly measuring herself against the accomplishments of her colleagues. It wasn't until she started journaling, pouring her anxieties and aspirations onto the page, that she began to understand the root of her insecurities. She realized that her desire for approval stemmed from her childhood experiences, where she felt pressured to conform to her parents' expectations. Through this process of introspection, Ruhi found the courage to redefine success on her own terms, letting go of external validation and focusing on her own personal growth and fulfillment.

Raman, a middle-aged businessman in Mumbai, had always prioritized his career over everything else. He built a successful company but sacrificed relationships and personal well-being in the process. After experiencing a health scare, Raman was forced to confront his priorities. He began to question his relentless pursuit of success and the sacrifices he had made. Through therapy and mindfulness practices, he began to rediscover the joys of connection, the importance of self-care, and the beauty of life beyond the boardroom. He realized that true fulfillment wasn't about achieving a certain status or accumulating wealth; it was about finding balance and living a life aligned with his values.

Deepika, a homemaker in Delhi, found herself trapped in a monotonous routine, feeling disconnected from her own sense of self. She had dedicated her life to her family and home but felt a yearning for something more. Through a local women's empowerment group, Deepika discovered a passion for baking. She began to experiment with recipes, her creativity blossoming in the kitchen. Sharing her creations with her community, Deepika discovered a sense of purpose and a renewed connection with her own talents. The journey inward had led her to rediscover her own passion and her ability to contribute to the world.

These are just a few examples of how the journey inward can transform lives. It's a path that can be fraught with challenges, but it's also a path that can lead to profound self-understanding, emotional growth, and a richer, more fulfilling life.

Tools for Self-Reflection:

To embark on this journey, we need tools to navigate the depths of our own being. Here are a few practices that can guide us:

Journaling: Writing regularly, even for a few minutes each day, allows us to process our thoughts and feelings. It's a safe space to explore our anxieties, dreams, and aspirations without judgment.

Mindfulness Meditation: Through mindfulness, we learn to observe our thoughts and emotions without judgment. We cultivate a sense of present-moment awareness, allowing us to connect with our inner experiences with greater clarity.

Therapy: Talking to a trained professional can provide a safe and supportive environment to explore deep-seated issues, process past traumas, and develop healthier coping mechanisms.

Creative Expression: Whether through painting, writing, music, or dance, creative pursuits allow us to express the complexities of our inner world in a tangible form.

Connecting with Nature: Spending time in nature can be a powerful tool for self-reflection. The quiet beauty of the natural world can help us quiet the noise of our minds and connect with a sense of peace and wonder.

Seeking Mentorship or Guidance: Sharing our experiences with a trusted mentor or guide can provide valuable insights and support. It's helpful to have someone who can offer a different perspective and challenge our assumptions.

Accepting Imperfection:

One of the most important aspects of the journey inward is accepting ourselves fully, flaws and all. We are all a work in progress, constantly evolving and changing. Embracing our imperfections is not about settling for mediocrity; it's about recognizing our humanity and treating ourselves with kindness and compassion.

There will be times when we stumble, when we make mistakes, or when we feel lost. This is part of the process. It's through these challenges that we grow and learn. The journey inward is not about reaching a perfect destination; it's about the ongoing journey of self-discovery, growth, and acceptance.

Continuing the Journey:

The journey inward is not a one-time event; it's a lifelong process. As we grow and evolve, our understanding of ourselves will continue to deepen. We may find ourselves revisiting old wounds, challenging long-held beliefs, or embracing new perspectives. This is the beauty of life — its constant potential for change and transformation.

The journey inward is a journey of self-discovery, growth, and acceptance. It's a path that leads to a deeper understanding of ourselves, our potential, and our place in the world. It's a journey worth taking, for it's through this exploration that we begin to live a life truly aligned with our values, our aspirations, and our true selves.

Personal Narratives of Growth:

The journey of self-discovery is a personal odyssey, a voyage into the uncharted territories of our own minds and hearts. It is a path less traveled, often winding and unpredictable, yet undeniably rewarding. In this exploration, we confront our deepest fears, challenge ingrained beliefs, and embrace the potential that lies dormant within us.

Let's delve into the stories of individuals who dared to embark on this transformative journey, their narratives echoing the universal struggles and triumphs that define the human experience.

Anya's Story: Embracing a New Chapter

Anya, a talented artist trapped in a mundane office job, found herself yearning for a life filled with creativity and purpose. The weight of societal expectations, the whispers of "practicality" and "security," had kept her chained to a path that stifled her spirit. But a spark of courage ignited within her. One evening, after a particularly soul-crushing day, she decided to paint. The brush felt like an extension of her own soul, and the canvas became a mirror reflecting her deepest desires. With each stroke, Anya felt a sense of liberation, a rediscovering of her true self. She began to explore her passion, enrolling in evening classes, seeking mentorship, and finding a community of artists who embraced her unique vision.

Anya's journey wasn't without its challenges. She faced doubts, anxieties, and moments of self-questioning. But fueled by a burning desire to live authentically, she persisted. The transition wasn't easy, but with each step, she gained confidence, resilience, and a renewed sense of purpose. She began to exhibit her work, attracting the attention of galleries and patrons. Her art became a testament to her resilience, a reflection of the courage she had summoned to break free from the confines of a life that no longer served her.

Pavan's Transformation: From Conformity to Authenticity

Pavan, a young man raised in a traditional Indian family, felt the pressure of expectations weighing heavily on his shoulders. He was expected to pursue a career in medicine or engineering, paths deemed respectable and secure. But his heart yearned for something different, something that ignited his passions. Pavan found solace in music, his fingers dancing across the piano keys, his voice soaring with emotion. But the fear of disapproval, the weight of societal norms, held him back. He kept his passion a secret, a hidden flame burning within.

One day, a chance encounter with a renowned musician sparked a flicker of hope. The musician, recognizing the raw talent in Pavan, encouraged him to pursue his dreams, regardless of the obstacles. This encounter became a turning point in Pavan's life. He decided to defy the expectations, to step out of the "brackets" that had confined him for so long. He enrolled in a music program, honed his skills, and eventually, shared his music with the world.

Pavan's journey wasn't without its sacrifices. He faced resistance from his family, the disapproval of his peers, and the occasional sting of societal judgment. But he remained steadfast, his passion driving him forward. His music, a testament to his resilience and authenticity, resonated with listeners, proving that breaking free from imposed limitations could lead to a truly fulfilling life.

Saumya's Awakening: Finding Strength Within

Saumya, a young woman burdened by societal expectations and self-doubt, found herself trapped in a cycle of comparison and dissatisfaction. She constantly measured herself against others, comparing her achievements, her looks, her life, feeling inadequate in the face of perceived perfection. This relentless self-criticism chipped away at her confidence, leaving her feeling lost and directionless. Saumya, yearning for a sense of belonging, searched for validation in external sources, seeking approval and acceptance from those around her.

One day, while attending a yoga retreat, Saumya stumbled upon a session focused on mindfulness and self-acceptance. Through meditation and introspection, she began to peel back the layers of self-doubt, uncovering a wellspring of strength and resilience within herself. She realized that true happiness and fulfillment were not to be found in external validation, but rather in cultivating a deep connection with her own inner self.

Saumya embarked on a journey of self-discovery, exploring her passions, embracing her strengths, and accepting her imperfections. She began to see the beauty in her uniqueness, the strength in her vulnerability, and the value in her own experiences. Her journey was a testament to the power of self-acceptance, a reminder that true worth comes from within, not from external sources.

The Power of Personal Narratives

These stories, though unique in their details, are woven together by a common thread: the transformative power of self-discovery. They remind us that the journey of breaking free from limitations is not about achieving perfection or becoming someone else. It is about embracing our authentic selves, accepting our imperfections, and living a life that resonates with our true values and aspirations.

The individuals in these narratives found strength in their vulnerability, courage in their fears, and inspiration in their own journeys. They taught us that self-discovery is a lifelong pursuit, a process of continuous growth and transformation. By embracing the unknown, by stepping outside our comfort zones, and by challenging the "brackets" that confine us, we unlock the boundless potential that lies within each of us.

147

The power of personal narratives lies in their ability to resonate with our own experiences, to offer hope and inspiration, and to remind us that we are not alone in our struggles. They provide a roadmap, a blueprint for navigating the complexities of life, offering guidance and encouragement along the way.

The adventure of self-discovery is not a solitary journey. We are surrounded by a community of individuals who have also faced their own challenges, who have also embarked on their own quests for growth and fulfillment. By sharing our stories, we build bridges of empathy and understanding, creating a tapestry of interconnected experiences that enrich our lives and inspire us to live more authentically.

<u>Tools for Self-Reflection:</u>

The journey of self-discovery is a lifelong adventure, an inward exploration that unveils the complexities of our being. It's a process of peeling back layers of conditioning, beliefs, and societal expectations to uncover our authentic selves. This chapter serves as a guide to embark on this introspective voyage, equipping you with tools and practices to navigate the intricate paths of self-understanding.

Imagine a vast, uncharted territory, a landscape within ourselves waiting to be explored. This internal landscape is where our deepest fears, desires, and aspirations reside. The path to self-discovery is akin to a quest, a journey of navigating this internal terrain, unearthing hidden truths, and embracing the fullness of who we are.

Self-reflection, the cornerstone of this adventure, is a deliberate act of turning inward, of examining our thoughts, feelings, and experiences with a non-judgmental lens. It's about pausing amidst the whirlwind of daily life, stepping back from the external world, and delving into the depths of our own consciousness.

Here are some practical tools to embark on your self-reflection journey:

1. Journaling

Journaling is a potent tool for introspection. It's a private space where we can pour out our thoughts, emotions, and experiences without the fear of judgment. By putting pen to paper, we externalize our internal world, making it easier to analyze and understand.

Prompts for Journaling:

What are my core values?

What brings me joy?

What are my fears and insecurities?

What are my strengths and weaknesses?

What are my dreams and aspirations?

What are my thoughts about specific events, relationships, or experiences?

What are the patterns I notice in my thoughts, emotions, and behaviors?

Types of Journaling:

Free Flow: Write whatever comes to mind without censoring yourself.

Gratitude Journal: Focus on listing things you're grateful for each day.

Dream Journal: Record your dreams upon waking to explore their symbolism.

Bullet Journal: Use a structured format to track goals, ideas, and reflections.

2. Meditation

Meditation is a powerful practice for quieting the mind and cultivating mindfulness. It allows us to step back from the constant chatter of our thoughts and observe them with detachment. By cultivating awareness, we gain insights into our mental patterns and emotional responses.

Types of Meditation:

Mindfulness Meditation: Focusing on the present moment, observing sensations, thoughts, and emotions without judgment.

Guided Meditation: Following a guided voice or audio that leads you through a specific meditation practice.

Transcendental Meditation: Repeating a mantra to transcend thoughts and experience inner stillness.

3. Mindfulness

Mindfulness is the practice of paying attention to the present moment without judgment. It's about being fully engaged with our experiences, whether it's the sensation of our breath, the taste of our food, or the feeling of the sun on our skin. By being present, we cultivate a deeper awareness of ourselves and our surroundings.

Mindfulness Practices:

Body Scan: Bringing awareness to different parts of your body, noticing sensations.

Mindful Walking: Focusing on the sensations of walking, the movement of your feet, and the environment around you.

Mindful Eating: Paying full attention to the process of eating, savoring flavors, and noticing textures.

4. Nature Walks

Nature has an inherent power to soothe the mind and inspire introspection. A quiet walk in a park, by the beach, or in the woods can be a transformative experience. The beauty and tranquility of nature can help us find clarity, connect with our inner selves, and gain fresh perspectives.

Nature Walk Practices:

Observing: Pay attention to the sights, sounds, and smells of the environment.

Contemplating: Reflect on your thoughts, feelings, and experiences as you walk.

Connecting: Feel a sense of connection with the natural world.

5. Shadow Work

Shadow work is a deep dive into the darker aspects of our psyche. It's about confronting our negative emotions, fears, and suppressed desires, acknowledging their existence, and integrating them into our conscious awareness. By acknowledging and accepting these shadow aspects, we can release their hold on us and become more whole.

Shadow Work Practices:

Journaling: Write about your negative emotions, fears, and repressed desires.

Meditation: Focus on your negative emotions, observing them without judgment.

Therapy: Work with a therapist to explore and understand your shadow aspects.

6. Feedback and Reflection

Seeking feedback from others can provide valuable insights into our blind spots. Ask friends, family members, or colleagues for honest feedback about our strengths, weaknesses, and areas for growth. Listen to their perspectives with an open mind and reflect on what you hear.

Feedback and Reflection Practices:

Asking for feedback: Be specific about the areas you want feedback on.

Active listening: Pay close attention to the feedback you receive.

Reflecting: Consider the feedback and how it applies to your life.

7. Creative Expression

Art, music, writing, dance, and other forms of creative expression can be powerful tools for self-discovery. They allow us to process our emotions, explore our inner world, and communicate our unique perspectives.

Creative Expression Practices:

Writing: Write poems, stories, essays, or journal entries.

Art: Paint, draw, sculpt, or create other forms of visual art.

Music: Play an instrument, sing, or listen to music that resonates with you.

Dance: Move your body freely and express yourself through dance.

8. Asking Questions

Self-reflection is often triggered by asking ourselves meaningful questions. These questions can be thought-provoking, challenging, or simply curious. They can lead us down paths of self-discovery we might not have considered otherwise.

Self-Reflection Questions:

What are my values, beliefs, and assumptions about life?

How do these values, beliefs, and assumptions affect my choices?

What am I afraid of?

What am I passionate about?

What brings me joy and fulfillment?

What do I want to achieve in life?

What are my strengths and weaknesses?

What are my patterns of thought, behavior, and emotion?

How can I be more authentically myself?

9. Embracing Imperfection

A vital part of self-discovery is accepting ourselves, flaws and all. We are not perfect beings. We have weaknesses, make mistakes, and have moments of self-doubt. Embracing our imperfections is a sign of self-compassion and acceptance. It allows us to be more forgiving of ourselves and others.

Embracing Imperfection Practices:

Challenge negative self-talk: Catch yourself when you're being critical of yourself and replace those thoughts with self-compassionate ones.

Practice self-acceptance: Recognize your strengths and weaknesses, and acknowledge that you are enough just as you are.

Focus on progress, not perfection: Celebrate your accomplishments, no matter how small.

10. Continuing the Journey

Self-discovery is not a destination, but a lifelong journey. It's a continuous process of growth, learning, and self-reflection. There will be times when we feel like we've reached a level of understanding, only to discover new layers to explore. Embrace the journey, for it is in the process of exploration that we discover the true meaning of self.

Continuing the Journey Practices:

Make self-reflection a regular practice: Set aside time each day or week for introspection.

Seek out new experiences: Step out of your comfort zone and try new things.

Connect with others: Share your journey with trusted friends, family, or a therapist.

By incorporating these tools and practices into your daily life, you can embark on the transformative adventure of self-discovery. The path may be winding and challenging, but the rewards are immense: a deeper understanding of yourself, a greater sense of purpose, and a more fulfilling life. Remember, the journey inwards is a journey worth taking, for it leads to a more authentic, empowered, and joyful version of yourself.

Accepting Imperfection:

The path to self-discovery is not a linear one, paved with smooth, predictable steps. It's more like a winding jungle trail, full of unexpected twists and turns, challenging climbs, and breathtaking vistas. Just as a hiker learns to appreciate the beauty and resilience of the forest by navigating its complexities, so too must we embrace the imperfections that make us human.

We often strive for perfection, yearning to present a polished, flaw-free image of ourselves to the world. But this relentless pursuit of flawlessness can be a trap, leading to self-criticism, anxiety, and a sense of inadequacy. We end up living in a state of constant self-judgment, afraid to let our true selves shine through.

Think of a beautifully handcrafted clay pot. The potter shapes the clay with care, but imperfections are part of the process. Cracks, uneven edges, and subtle variations in glaze add to the pot's character and uniqueness. The imperfections tell a story, reflecting the artist's touch, the journey of the clay, and the resilience of the final piece.

In the same way, our imperfections are not flaws to be concealed but facets of our being that contribute to our rich and complex tapestry. They tell a story of our experiences, our struggles, and our triumphs. They are the scars that mark our resilience, the wrinkles that reflect our wisdom, the stumbles that have taught us valuable lessons.

Accepting these imperfections is an act of self-love, a recognition of our humanity. It's about embracing the totality of who we are, flaws and all.

This acceptance allows us to release the pressure of constant self-improvement and to truly appreciate the uniqueness of our journey.

Consider the Indian tradition of "pattachitra," a vibrant form of scroll painting. The artists meticulously depict scenes from mythology and folklore, often using bright colors and intricate details. However, they don't shy away from imperfections. The brushstrokes may be slightly uneven, the lines might not be perfectly straight, and the colors might have subtle variations. Yet, these imperfections don't detract from the beauty and power of the artwork. They add to its authenticity and charm, reminding us that human creation is never perfect, but always unique.

In our own lives, we too can embrace the imperfections of our stories. We can stop trying to erase the blemishes and instead focus on the beauty of our individuality. We can learn to appreciate the quirks, the flaws, and the imperfections that make us uniquely us.

This acceptance doesn't mean we stop striving for growth. It means we embrace the journey, with all its complexities and inconsistencies, as part of the process of self-discovery. It's about finding the beauty and strength in our imperfections, learning to love ourselves, flaws and all.

Here are some practical steps to help you embrace your imperfections:

Acknowledge Your Flaws: Instead of trying to hide them, acknowledge them. Recognize that they are part of what makes you unique.

Challenge Negative Thoughts: When you catch yourself criticizing yourself, challenge those thoughts. Ask yourself, "Is this truly accurate? Is this helping me grow?"

Focus on Your Strengths: Dwell on your positive attributes and the things you do well. This will help balance out the negative self-talk.

Surround Yourself with Supportive People: Seek out individuals who appreciate and accept you for who you are. Their positive energy can be a powerful antidote to self-criticism.

Practice Self-Compassion: Treat yourself with kindness and understanding, just as you would a close friend. Be patient with yourself as you navigate the journey of self-acceptance.

Embracing imperfections is not about accepting mediocrity. It's about embracing the totality of your experience, the good, the bad, and the messy. It's about recognizing that your flaws don't define you; they are part of what makes you beautiful, resilient, and uniquely you.

This journey of self-acceptance is not a destination but a lifelong exploration. It's about learning to navigate the complexities of your being, celebrating your strengths, and finding grace in your imperfections. It's about recognizing that true self-love lies in accepting yourself, flaws and all, and allowing yourself to shine.

<u>Continuing the Journey:</u>

The journey of self-discovery is not a sprint, but a marathon. It's a continuous exploration of the inner landscape, a quest for understanding who we are at our core, and what makes us tick. It's a process that unfolds throughout life, evolving with each experience, each encounter, and each challenge we face. It's about shedding the layers of conditioning, the beliefs and expectations that have been imposed upon us, and embracing the authentic self that lies beneath.

The road to self-discovery is not always smooth. It's paved with moments of self-doubt, moments of uncertainty, and moments of vulnerability. But it's precisely these moments that offer the greatest opportunities for growth. It's in these moments of introspection, of questioning and challenging our own perceptions, that we begin to unravel the intricate tapestry of our own being.

> Imagine a young woman named **Aneri**, a budding artist from a small town in India. She dreamed of pursuing a career in art, but the societal expectations placed upon her were immense. Her family, her community, and even her own internalized beliefs told her that a woman's place was in the home, not in the unpredictable world of art. Anjali felt a constant pull between her dreams and the expectations that surrounded her. She felt trapped, like a bird in a cage, yearning to break free but afraid of the consequences.

The journey of self-discovery often begins with a quiet whisper, a spark of dissatisfaction with the status quo. Aneri found her whisper in a chance encounter with a renowned artist during a family trip to a larger city. The artist's passion, her unwavering belief in her own artistic vision, ignited a fire in Aneri's heart. It was a moment of revelation, a realization that she couldn't ignore her own calling.

The path to self-discovery rarely leads to a destination; it's a journey of constant exploration and evolution. Aneri's journey was no different. She started by enrolling in online art classes, venturing outside her comfort zone, and stepping into the unknown. She faced resistance from her family, their disapproval a constant reminder of the societal norms she was challenging. But Aneri's determination grew with each brushstroke, with each piece of art that poured her emotions onto the canvas.

As she delved deeper into her artistic passion, Aneri began to question the beliefs that had shaped her identity. She challenged the notion that a woman's role was solely confined to the home. She started to see her family's expectations not as limitations, but as opportunities for understanding. Through open communication and honest conversations, she began to bridge the gap between her dreams and her family's fears.

This journey wasn't about rebelling or defying societal norms; it was about understanding her own desires and finding a way to reconcile them with the expectations of her world. Aneri discovered that true self-discovery involves a delicate balance between embracing one's individuality and acknowledging the context in which one lives.

Aneri's journey wasn't a smooth sail. She faced moments of doubt, moments of fear, and moments of isolation. But she learned to navigate these challenges by building a strong support system of friends, mentors, and online communities who shared her passion. She found solace in the camaraderie of other artists, exchanging ideas, receiving feedback, and drawing inspiration from their journeys.

Self-discovery often involves dismantling the walls we build around ourselves, the barriers we erect to protect ourselves from the perceived judgment of others. For Aneri, it was a constant process of letting go of the need for external validation. She began to value her own artistic vision, embracing her unique perspective and style, even if it wasn't always understood by everyone around her.

The journey of self-discovery is a lifelong adventure. It's about continually challenging our own perceptions, embracing our strengths and weaknesses, and learning to navigate the complexities of our own being. It's a journey of self-acceptance, a process of learning to love ourselves unconditionally, flaws and all.

Aneri's journey is a testament to the power of self-discovery. It's a reminder that we are not defined by societal expectations or external validation. We are architects of our own lives, with the power to shape our destinies and create a life that is authentically ours.

The pursuit of self-discovery is not a destination, but a continuous process of growth, evolution, and self-acceptance. It's a journey that requires courage, resilience, and a willingness to embrace the unknown. It's a journey that begins within, a journey that leads us to a deeper understanding of ourselves, and ultimately, to a life that is truly fulfilling.

Like Aneri, each of us has a unique story to tell, a journey of self-discovery waiting to unfold. The journey may be challenging, but it's also immensely rewarding. It's a journey worth taking, a journey that leads us to a more authentic and fulfilling life.

So, embark on your own adventure of self-discovery. Explore the depths of your own being, challenge your beliefs, embrace your individuality, and never stop learning and growing. The world needs your unique voice, your unique perspective, and your unique contribution to the tapestry of life.

8

THE EMPOWERMENT OF EMPATHY

<u>The Role of Empathy in Relationships:</u>

Empathy plays a crucial role in fostering healthy and fulfilling relationships. From a psychological perspective, empathy allows us to understand and share the feelings of our partners, creating a sense of connection and intimacy.

This shared understanding fosters trust and strengthens bonds, while a lack of empathy can lead to misunderstandings and conflict.

Sociologically, empathy promotes social cohesion by encouraging cooperation and compassion, fostering a sense of community within the relationship. However, some argue that empathy can be detrimental, leading to emotional overwhelm or manipulation. This viewpoint emphasizes the importance of boundaries and self-awareness in navigating empathy.

Ultimately, the role of empathy in relationships is multifaceted, requiring a delicate balance of understanding, compassion, and self-preservation.

The concept of empathy and its role in relationships is a delicate and multifaceted one. It can be a powerful tool for fostering deep and meaningful connections, but it must be navigated with care and awareness.

This was a lesson that **Anamika** was learning the hard way.

> Anamika had always prided herself on her empathetic nature. She was the friend that everyone came to for advice and support, and

she wore her heart on her sleeve. When she met her partner, Jay, she was immediately drawn to his charming and charismatic personality. He seemed to have a natural empathy for others, and their connection was instant.

However, as their relationship progressed, Anamika began to notice a disturbing pattern. Jay's empathy seemed to have an 'off' switch, and when he became angry or frustrated, his ability to understand and share her feelings disappeared. Their once intimate connection felt one-sided, and Anamika found herself walking on eggshells, afraid of triggering his temper. It was a challenging realization for Anamika that her natural empathy, which had always been her strength, was now being used against her.

She loved Jay and wanted to believe that their relationship was special and unique, as he often reminded her. But the warning signs were there, and Anamika began to question if her empathy was clouding her judgment. Was she ignoring red flags because of her deep desire to understand and help him? Had her empathy become a tool for manipulation? These were difficult questions that kept her up at night, as she grappled with the complex role of empathy in her relationship.

<u>Stories of Compassion in Action:</u>

Empathy has the power to bridge divides, mend hearts, and create a more compassionate world. It is the bedrock of meaningful connections, fostering understanding and a sense of shared humanity. In the tapestry of human experience, countless acts of empathy have left an indelible mark on individuals and communities alike. These stories, often untold, reveal the transformative nature of compassion and its ability to inspire profound change.

Let's delve into the lives of ordinary people who, through acts of empathy, have made an extraordinary difference:

The Teacher Who Believed in Second Chances:

In the bustling streets of Mumbai, amidst the cacophony of urban life, resided a dedicated teacher named **Mrs. Joshi**. Her classroom was a sanctuary for children from diverse backgrounds, many of whom faced immense challenges. One such student, **Sunil**, struggled with behavioral issues and academic difficulties. He was often labelled a troublemaker, a tag that seemed to follow him like a shadow. However, Mrs. Joshi refused to let Sunil's past define him.

She saw beneath the surface, recognizing the pain and frustration fueling his actions. With patience and unwavering belief, she nurtured his potential. She created a safe space for him to express his emotions, providing him with the individual attention he craved. Slowly, Sunil began to respond to her kindness. The anger that had once clouded his demeanor gradually gave way to a glimmer of hope. He started engaging in class, his curiosity piqued by Mrs. Joshi's passionate lessons.

The transformation was remarkable. Sunil, once a troubled youth, blossomed into a responsible and engaged student. His academic performance soared, and he developed a newfound respect for himself and others. This was all thanks to the empathy of a teacher who refused to give up on him.

The Neighbor Who Offered a Helping Hand:

In the tranquil village of Madurai, nestled amidst lush paddy fields, lived an elderly woman named **Tara**. She had always been known for her warm smile and generous spirit. One evening, as she was preparing dinner, she noticed a commotion outside her humble dwelling. A young couple, new to the village, had arrived with their newborn baby, but their car had broken down, leaving them stranded and without any support.

Without hesitation, Tara extended a warm invitation to the couple, offering them shelter and comfort. She prepared a nourishing meal and provided them with clean clothes and bedding. She even contacted a local mechanic to assist with their car. The couple, overwhelmed by her kindness, was deeply moved by her selfless act. They had arrived in a foreign land, feeling lost and vulnerable, but Tara's compassion made them feel welcomed and cared for.

Tara's simple gesture of empathy had a profound impact on the couple. It not only offered them immediate relief but also forged a lasting bond. Word of her kindness spread through the village, reminding everyone of the power of human connection.

The Activist Who Championed Inclusion:

In the heart of Delhi, a passionate young activist named **Seema** dedicated her life to advocating for the rights of people with disabilities. Inspired by her own experiences, she saw firsthand the challenges and prejudices faced by those with physical limitations. She recognized the systemic barriers that prevented them from accessing equal opportunities.

Seema's empathy for this marginalized community fueled her tireless efforts. She organized awareness campaigns, lobbied for inclusive policies, and worked tirelessly to create accessible environments. She collaborated with architects, policymakers, and community leaders to break down barriers and ensure equal access to education, healthcare, and employment.

Seema's dedication brought about tangible change. The lives of countless people with disabilities were transformed through her advocacy. Her actions not only empowered them but also fostered a more inclusive society where everyone felt valued and respected.

The Power of Empathy in the Face of Adversity:

These stories, though diverse in their contexts, all share a common thread: the transformative power of empathy. In times of crisis and uncertainty, acts of compassion can provide solace, hope, and a sense of shared humanity.

During the COVID-19 pandemic, when the world faced an unprecedented health crisis, countless individuals stepped up to help their fellow human beings. Healthcare workers tirelessly risked their own safety to care for the sick. Communities came together to support those in need, offering food, shelter, and emotional support.

The pandemic highlighted the interconnectedness of humanity and underscored the vital role of empathy in navigating difficult times. It served as a poignant reminder that compassion is not simply an abstract ideal but a powerful force that can shape our world for the better.

The Ripple Effect of Kindness:

Acts of empathy often have a ripple effect, extending far beyond the initial interaction. When one person extends a helping hand, it can inspire others to do the same, creating a chain reaction of compassion.

A small gesture of kindness, such as offering a smile or listening attentively, can make a world of difference to someone struggling with loneliness or despair. These seemingly insignificant acts can have a profound impact, restoring a sense of hope and reminding individuals that they are not alone.

Cultivating an Empathetic Mindset:

Developing an empathetic mindset is a journey of self-awareness and compassion. It involves actively listening to others, understanding their perspectives, and recognizing their feelings. It requires acknowledging the shared humanity that binds us all, despite our differences.

Here are some ways to cultivate empathy in our daily lives:

Practice active listening: Pay attention to what others are saying, both verbally and nonverbally. Try to understand their feelings and perspectives.

Challenge biases: Recognize and confront our own prejudices and assumptions. Make an effort to learn from people with different backgrounds and experiences.

Engage in acts of kindness: Look for opportunities to help others, even in small ways. A simple act of kindness can make a significant difference in someone's life.

Practice gratitude: Focusing on the good in our lives can cultivate a more compassionate outlook. Expressing gratitude to others for their contributions can strengthen relationships.

The World We Can Create:

Empathy is not just a personal virtue; it is a fundamental building block of a just and equitable society. When we cultivate empathy, we create a more inclusive and compassionate world where everyone feels valued and respected.

The stories of compassion in action remind us that even in the face of adversity, there is always hope. By embracing empathy, we can transform our lives and the lives of others, building a brighter future for all.

<u>Cultivating an Empathetic Mindset:</u>

Empathy is a profound and powerful emotion that allows us to connect deeply with others, understand their experiences, and share in their joys and sorrows. It's a bridge that transcends the boundaries of our own individual perceptions and opens our hearts to the richness of human experience. Yet, in a world that often prioritizes individuality and self-interest, cultivating empathy can be a challenging endeavor. But it's a journey worth undertaking, for empathy is not just a virtue; it's a transformative force that enriches our lives, strengthens our relationships, and fosters a more compassionate and understanding world.

Imagine a world where we truly listened to each other, where we sought to understand perspectives different from our own, where we acknowledged the shared humanity that binds us all. This is the world that empathy can create. It's a world where kindness and compassion flourish, where differences are celebrated, and where we recognize the interconnectedness of our lives.

To cultivate empathy, we must first understand its essence. It's more than just feeling sorry for someone or simply acknowledging their emotions. True empathy involves actively stepping into another person's shoes, trying to see the world through their eyes, and understanding their motivations, beliefs, and experiences. It requires a willingness to suspend our own judgments and biases and to open ourselves to the possibility that another person's reality may be different from our own.

But cultivating empathy doesn't happen overnight. It requires conscious effort, a willingness to learn, and a commitment to ongoing self-reflection. Here are a few strategies that can help us develop an empathetic mindset:

1. Practice Active Listening:

Active listening is a fundamental skill in developing empathy. It's about truly hearing what another person is saying, both verbally and nonverbally. This involves paying attention to their tone of voice, body language, and facial expressions. It's also about asking clarifying questions and reflecting back what you've heard to ensure you understand their perspective.

2. Seek to Understand Diverse Perspectives:

Challenge your own biases and assumptions. Engage with different viewpoints, even those that challenge your own beliefs. This might involve reading books, watching documentaries, or having conversations with people from diverse backgrounds. Step outside of your comfort zone and expose yourself to perspectives that broaden your understanding of the world.

3. Embrace Curiosity and Ask Open-Ended Questions:

Approach conversations with a genuine curiosity about the other person's experiences. Instead of focusing on your own thoughts and opinions, ask open-ended questions that encourage them to share their stories, perspectives, and feelings.

4. Practice Mirroring and Validation:

Mirroring involves reflecting back the other person's emotions and verbal cues, while validation is acknowledging the legitimacy of their feelings. Both are crucial for building trust and understanding. Saying something like, "It sounds like you're feeling really frustrated right now," or "I understand why you might be feeling that way" can go a long way in creating a sense of connection.

5. Develop Emotional Intelligence:

Emotional intelligence is the ability to understand and manage our own emotions as well as those of others. It involves self-awareness, self-regulation, empathy, and social skills. By developing our emotional intelligence, we can better navigate complex social interactions and respond with compassion and understanding.

6. Practice Mindfulness and Compassion:

Mindfulness is about being present in the moment and observing our thoughts, feelings, and sensations without judgment. It helps us cultivate awareness of our own emotions and those of others. Compassion involves extending kindness and care to ourselves and others, recognizing our shared humanity.

7. Engage in Acts of Kindness:

Kindness is a powerful expression of empathy. Small acts of kindness, like helping a neighbor, offering a listening ear, or simply smiling at a stranger, can have a ripple effect, creating a more positive and connected world.

8. Embrace Vulnerability and Share Your Own Stories:

Vulnerability is key to building authentic connections. It involves being open and honest about our own experiences, feelings, and struggles. Sharing our own vulnerabilities can create a sense of safety and understanding, allowing others to feel seen and heard.

Cultivating empathy is a journey, not a destination. It's a lifelong process of learning, growing, and challenging ourselves to see the world through the eyes of others. As we develop our capacity for empathy, we unlock a profound sense of connection, enriching our own lives and creating a more compassionate and understanding world for all.

Empathy and Community Building:

Empathy, the ability to understand and share the feelings of another, is not merely a personal virtue but a powerful force that can bind communities together. It acts as a bridge, connecting individuals across differences, fostering understanding, and nurturing a sense of belonging.

Imagine a bustling neighborhood in Mumbai. The aroma of chai wafts through the air, blending with the sounds of laughter and chatter. While this scene might seem like a picture of harmonious coexistence, it's often the subtle acts of empathy that truly bind this community together.

Take, for instance, the elderly woman who lives alone. She often finds it difficult to carry her groceries home, especially during the monsoon season. Her neighbor, a young boy named **Rohan**, observes this struggle. He doesn't simply look away; he sees her need and offers to help. Rohan's act of empathy isn't just about lending a hand; it's about showing compassion and understanding. It reinforces a sense of community, demonstrating that even small gestures can have a significant impact.

In another corner of the neighborhood, a group of women gather to discuss their daily lives. One of them, **Anita**, shares her anxieties about her son's upcoming exams. Instead of offering generic advice, the women listen attentively, offering words of encouragement and sharing their own experiences with exams. Their shared understanding and empathy create a supportive space where Anita feels heard and understood.

These seemingly small acts of empathy weave a tapestry of connection, creating a strong and resilient community. But the power of empathy goes beyond mere acts of kindness. It lies in the ability to see beyond surface-level differences and recognize the shared humanity that binds us all.

Consider the case of a young woman, **Meera**, who recently moved from a small village to the city. Meera feels lost and overwhelmed by the sheer scale of the city's hustle and bustle. She finds it difficult to adjust to the pace and the anonymity of urban life. However, when she joins a local community group, she finds a sense of belonging.

Within this group, Meera discovers a diverse mix of individuals: an elderly gentleman who shares his stories of the city's past, a young entrepreneur who talks about her struggles and triumphs, and a group of students who share their dreams and aspirations. Meera, initially apprehensive, begins to open up to these strangers. She discovers that despite their different backgrounds, they share similar anxieties, hopes, and dreams. This shared experience of vulnerability fosters a sense of empathy, creating a safe space for Meera to connect and grow.

The community group serves as a microcosm of the larger society. It teaches us that empathy is not just about understanding individual experiences but also about appreciating the unique tapestry of human emotions and aspirations that make up our communities. It's about seeing beyond the labels that often divide us and recognizing the common threads that bind us together.

Empathy can be a powerful tool for building strong communities. By fostering understanding, compassion, and connection, empathy can bridge cultural divides, promote social harmony, and create a sense of belonging for all. In a world often characterized by division and conflict, empathy offers a path toward unity and shared prosperity.

As we move beyond the boundaries of our comfort zones and embrace diversity, empathy becomes a crucial compass guiding us toward a more inclusive and compassionate world.

It's a journey we must undertake, not just individually but collectively. It's a journey that begins with recognizing the shared humanity that binds us, understanding the experiences of others, and taking the time to connect on a deeper level.

The act of empathy, seemingly small and insignificant, has the potential to create ripples of change that spread throughout our communities, shaping a more just and equitable future. Let's embrace the power of empathy and build a world where everyone feels truly seen, heard, and valued.

<u>The Ripple Effect of Kindness:</u>

The sun dipped below the horizon, casting long shadows across the bustling streets of Mumbai. As the city's energy shifted from the day's frenetic pace to the more relaxed rhythm of twilight, a sense of peace settled over a small, quiet bookstore nestled in a corner of Bandra. Inside, a young woman named **Tina** sat engrossed in a book, her brow furrowed in concentration. She was an avid reader, drawn to stories that explored the complexities of human emotions and the profound impact of relationships.

Tina had stumbled upon this particular book, "The Ripple Effect," just a few days ago, and its message had struck a chord within her. It spoke of the transformative power of empathy and how even the smallest acts of kindness could create a chain reaction of positive change. The book had sparked a flicker of hope in her, a yearning for something more, a desire to make a difference in the world around her.

As Tina delved deeper into the book, she was captivated by the stories of ordinary people who had made extraordinary choices, driven by their empathy for others. One such story was about a young street vendor named **Raju**, who lived in a small village in Uttar Pradesh. Raju was known for his generosity, always willing to share his meagre earnings with those less fortunate. One day, a devastating storm swept through his village, leaving many homes in ruins. Raju, despite having lost everything himself, rallied his neighbors, distributing food and shelter to those who had been affected.

His simple act of kindness, fueled by empathy, ignited a spark of hope in the hearts of his community. People who had been strangers before found themselves united in their shared experience of loss and their determination to rebuild. They worked together, supporting each other, finding strength in their shared humanity. Raju's selfless act had not just helped those in need, it had created a ripple effect of compassion that spread throughout the village.

Tina was deeply moved by Raju's story. It resonated with her own experiences, reminding her of the times she had hesitated to extend a helping hand, fearing it might not make a difference. The book had shown her that even the smallest acts of kindness could have a profound impact on the world around her.

As Tina continued reading, she came across another story, this time about a group of students in Bangalore who had launched a project to empower underprivileged children. These students, driven by their empathy for those less fortunate, had organized workshops, providing underprivileged children with access to education and opportunities. They had witnessed firsthand the power of education, the way it could transform lives and break cycles of poverty.

Their commitment to making a difference, driven by their empathy, had led them to create a ripple effect that extended far beyond their immediate community. They had inspired other young people to get involved, creating a movement of compassion that was changing lives.

These stories, and many others like them, reinforced the message that empathy was not just a feeling, but a powerful force for positive change. Tina began to see the world around her differently, noticing the small acts of kindness that were happening every day. She saw the elderly woman who offered a seat on the crowded bus to a pregnant woman, the young boy who shared his lunch with a classmate who had forgotten his, the shopkeeper who gave a discount to a customer who was struggling financially.

These seemingly insignificant acts, driven by empathy, were creating a ripple effect that was making a difference. Tina realized that she too could contribute to this wave of kindness. She started small, offering a helping hand to her neighbor who was recovering from an illness, volunteering at a local shelter for stray animals, and donating to charities that worked to alleviate poverty.

With each act of kindness, Tina felt a sense of fulfilment, a deeper connection to the world around her. She realized that empathy was not just about feeling compassion for others, it was about taking action, about making a tangible difference in the lives of those around her.

The book had awakened something within Tina, a dormant sense of purpose. It had shown her that even in the midst of a bustling, often indifferent city, there was room for kindness and compassion. The power of empathy, she realized, was not limited to grand gestures or monumental acts of heroism. It was found in the everyday, in the small acts of kindness that we often overlook.

As Tina closed the book, her heart was filled with a renewed sense of hope. She knew that she had a part to play in creating a world that was kinder, more compassionate, and more just. The book had shown her that the ripple effect of kindness could reach far and wide, transforming lives and communities, one act at a time.

Tina walked out of the bookstore; her spirit lifted by the message of "The

Ripple Effect." She knew that she had a responsibility to share this message with others, to inspire them to embrace the power of empathy and to create a world where kindness was not just a virtue, but a way of life.

As she walked along the crowded streets of Mumbai, Tina couldn't help but smile. She saw the world through new eyes, filled with a sense of possibility and purpose. She knew that the journey ahead would not be easy, but she was determined to do her part, to create her own ripple effect of kindness, and to make a difference in the world, one small act at a time.

The Ripple Effect of Kindness

The concept of the ripple effect is a powerful metaphor that captures the interconnectedness of our actions and their impact on the world around us. Just as a pebble dropped into a still pond creates ripples that spread outwards, so too do our acts of kindness, no matter how small, create a chain reaction that extends far beyond our immediate circle.

This concept is particularly relevant in India, a country with a rich tradition of compassion and generosity. The Indian culture values the importance of community, of looking after one another, and of extending a helping hand to those in need. Throughout history, India has witnessed countless examples of individuals and communities coming together to support each other, sharing resources, and offering comfort in times of adversity.

These acts of kindness, often born out of empathy and compassion, have created a ripple effect that has shaped the very fabric of Indian society. From the ancient practice of "annadana," the act of sharing food with the hungry, to the modern-day phenomenon of "Missionaries of Charity," dedicated to serving the poor and marginalized, Indian culture is steeped in the belief that acts of kindness have the power to heal, uplift, and transform.

The ripple effect of kindness can be seen in countless ways, from the everyday gestures of generosity that we witness in our communities to the larger movements that aim to address social issues. In the bustling cities and villages of India, we see countless examples of people extending a helping hand to those in need.

The elderly woman who offers her seat on the crowded bus to a pregnant woman, the young boy who shares his lunch with a classmate who has forgotten his, the shopkeeper who gives a discount to a customer struggling financially - these seemingly insignificant acts, driven by empathy, create a ripple effect that makes a difference in the lives of those around them.

These acts of kindness, however small, are not just about making someone's day a little brighter, they are about fostering a sense of community, of shared humanity, and of interconnectedness. They remind us that we are all part of a larger web of life, where our actions have consequences, both positive and negative.

The ripple effect of kindness can also be seen in the larger movements that aim to address social issues. In India, we have witnessed the rise of numerous NGOs and social enterprises dedicated to improving the lives of those less fortunate. These organizations are driven by a deep sense of empathy for the marginalized and a commitment to creating a more equitable and just society.

From empowering underprivileged children with education to providing healthcare to those living in poverty, these organizations are working tirelessly to create a ripple effect that extends to countless lives. They are challenging the status quo, breaking down barriers, and inspiring others to join them in their mission.

The power of the ripple effect is not limited to India. It is a universal truth that applies to all of us, regardless of our cultural background or geographic location. Every act of kindness, no matter how small, has the potential to create a chain reaction of positive change.

Embracing the Ripple Effect

In today's world, it's easy to become disillusioned, to feel overwhelmed by the negativity and suffering that we see around us. But the truth is that even in the midst of darkness, there is always hope, and the power of kindness is a potent force for good.

The ripple effect reminds us that we all have the power to make a difference, that our actions, no matter how small, can have a profound impact on the world around us. It encourages us to embrace empathy, to cultivate compassion, and to find ways to extend a helping hand to those in need.

Embracing the ripple effect is not just about doing good deeds for the sake of it, it's about recognizing the interconnectedness of all beings and the power of our actions to create a more just, compassionate, and equitable world. It's about understanding that our choices have consequences, that our lives are intertwined with the lives of others, and that we have a responsibility to use our gifts and talents to make a positive impact.

Here are some ways that we can embrace the ripple effect in our daily lives:

> **Practice active listening.** When someone is sharing their story, listen with genuine interest and empathy. Try to understand their perspective, even if you don't agree with it.

> **Offer a helping hand.** If you see someone struggling, offer to help, even if it's just a small gesture.

> **Be kind to yourself.** Self-compassion is essential for cultivating empathy for others. Treat yourself with kindness and understanding, and recognize your own strengths and weaknesses.

> **Support local charities.** Donating your time or money to organizations that work to address social issues can make a real difference in the lives of others.

Spread positivity. Choose to focus on the good in the world and share positive stories and messages with others.

By embracing the ripple effect, we can create a more compassionate, just, and equitable world. It's a journey that starts with ourselves, with our own willingness to extend kindness and empathy to those around us. It's a journey that is both personal and collective, one that requires us to be mindful of our actions and their impact on the world.

The ripple effect is a powerful reminder that we are all connected, that our choices matter, and that even the smallest act of kindness can make a world of difference. Let us all strive to be part of the wave of compassion, creating a ripple effect of kindness that extends to all corners of the globe.

9

THE COURAGE TO LIVE AUTHENTICALLY

<u>Understanding Authenticity:</u>

Living authentically is a journey of self-discovery, a quest to align our actions with our deepest values and beliefs. It's about shedding the masks we wear to please others and embracing the true essence of who we are, flaws and all. It's about living in harmony with our inner compass, making choices that resonate with our soul, and expressing ourselves with genuine vulnerability.

Imagine a tapestry woven with threads of societal expectations, familial pressures, and personal aspirations. Each thread represents a part of our identity, contributing to the intricate pattern of our lives. Living authentically involves untangling these threads, discerning which ones truly belong to us, and weaving a new tapestry that reflects our authentic self.

Often, we are taught to prioritize external validation, chasing societal ideals of success, happiness, and worthiness. We are told to follow a predefined script, embracing the roles and expectations imposed upon us. This creates a disconnect between who we are and who we believe we should be, leading to a life that feels unfulfilling and out of sync.

The path to authenticity begins with self-awareness, a willingness to look inward and confront our deepest fears, limiting beliefs, and unfulfilled desires. It requires courage to acknowledge our vulnerabilities, to embrace our imperfections, and to be honest with ourselves about what truly matters.

We are not defined by the labels society attaches to us or by the roles we play in life. We are not limited by our past mistakes or the judgments of others. Our true essence lies in the unique combination of thoughts, emotions, and experiences that make us who we are.

Living authentically doesn't mean being perfect or always making the right choices. It means being true to ourselves even when it's uncomfortable, even when it challenges our beliefs, and even when it means going against the grain. It means embracing the messiness of life, the contradictions, the imperfections, and the complexities of our human experience.

Here are some reflections to help you explore the meaning of authentic living:

What are your core values? These are the guiding principles that define your moral compass. Identify them and ask yourself whether your actions align with them.

What brings you joy? What activities ignite your passion? Do you spend enough time pursuing these interests?

What are your fears? What prevents you from being fully yourself? Examine these fears and find ways to overcome them.

What are your strengths and weaknesses? Embrace your strengths and acknowledge your weaknesses. This is where true self-acceptance begins.

What are your dreams? What are your aspirations for the future? Do your dreams align with your authentic self?

Living authentically is a journey of continuous growth and evolution. It's about constantly questioning our beliefs, challenging our assumptions, and staying true to ourselves even when it's difficult. It's about letting go of the need for external approval and embracing the freedom of being our own unique selves.

Here are some practical steps you can take to cultivate a more authentic life:

> **Practice self-reflection.** Regularly dedicate time to journaling, meditation, or simply quiet contemplation. These practices help you connect with your inner self and gain clarity on your values and desires.

> **Seek support from trusted friends and family.** Share your journey with people who understand and support you. Their encouragement and perspective can help you stay on track.

> **Embrace your passions.** Make time for activities that bring you joy and fulfillment. Don't let your passions fade due to busyness or fear of judgment.

> **Challenge limiting beliefs.** Identify the beliefs that hold you back and question their validity. Start by challenging one limiting belief at a time.

> **Express yourself creatively.** Explore your creativity through writing, painting, music, or any art form that speaks to your soul.

> **Live with intention.** Make conscious choices that align with your values and goals. Ask yourself: "Does this action reflect who I truly am?"

> **Be kind to yourself.** Embrace your imperfections and celebrate your uniqueness. Treat yourself with the same compassion and kindness you would extend to others.

Remember, living authentically is an ongoing process. It's not about reaching a destination but about embracing the journey itself. It's about continually striving to live in alignment with our truest selves, embracing the complexities and contradictions of life, and finding joy in the simple act of being who we are.

The path to authenticity is not always easy. There will be moments of doubt, fear, and resistance. But with perseverance, self-compassion, and a willingness to embrace vulnerability, you can create a life that feels truly fulfilling and aligned with your authentic self.

Authenticity is not a destination, but a journey. It's a constant process of self-discovery, self-acceptance, and living in alignment with our values. It's about shedding the masks we wear to please others and embracing the beautiful, messy, complex truth of who we truly are. It's about finding our voice, expressing our truth, and living a life that feels authentic, meaningful, and truly ours.

Stories of Authentic Living:

The stories we share in this chapter are not fairy tales, but real-life narratives of individuals who dared to step out of the shadows and embrace their authentic selves. They are stories of individuals who chose to live life on their own terms, defying societal norms and internalized pressures. These are not tales of overnight transformations, but journeys paved with courage, self-discovery, and unwavering dedication to their truest selves.

> Let's begin with the story of **Lesha**, a young woman from a conservative family in Delhi. From a young age, Lesha felt a strong pull towards the world of art, but her family, steeped in traditional values, deemed it an impractical career choice. The pressure to pursue a stable, "respectable" profession like medicine or engineering was immense. Lesha felt the weight of expectations bearing down on her, and she struggled to reconcile her passion with the desires of her family. Yet, Lesha refused to be silenced.

She enrolled in a prestigious medical college, as her family wished, but she never truly abandoned her love for art. Secretly, she took evening classes in painting, attending workshops, and pouring her heart into her canvases. Her passion burned bright, a quiet rebellion against the confines of her seemingly pre-determined life.

Years passed, Lesha graduated with honors, fulfilling the expectations of her family. But deep down, her heart yearned for something more, something authentically her own. Finally, after much deliberation, she shared her artistic aspirations with her family. The response was not as harsh as she feared. While her parents were initially apprehensive, they saw the passion in her eyes, the fire in her spirit. They eventually relented, understanding that true happiness lay in following one's own path.

Embracing the courage she had always possessed, Lesha quit her medical career, focusing entirely on her art. She started painting full-time, her canvases bursting with vibrant colors and raw emotion. Her talent was soon recognized, leading to exhibitions, commissions, and a blossoming artistic career. Lesha's story is not just about the pursuit of artistic dreams, but about the courage to be true to oneself, even in the face of societal expectations. She demonstrated that a fulfilling life can be built on the foundation of authenticity, a life where your passions fuel your path.

> Another inspiring story is that of **Akash**, a young man from Mumbai who, despite growing up in a privileged family, felt stifled by societal expectations. He was expected to follow in the footsteps of his father, a successful businessman, and take over the family enterprise. But Akash yearned for a life of meaning, one that transcended the pursuit of material wealth.

Akash felt a deep connection to the environment, a love for nature that his family dismissed as a fleeting passion. He felt a strong urge to contribute to conservation efforts, to make a difference in the world. The pressure to conform, to live up to his family's expectations, weighed heavily on his mind. But Akash refused to compromise his own values.

He decided to pursue a degree in environmental science, defying the wishes of his family. His decision was met with resistance, his family struggling to understand his choice. They saw it as a betrayal of their legacy, a disregard for their sacrifices. But Akash stood his ground, choosing to live a life aligned with his own values.

He dedicated himself to his studies, working tirelessly to create a life he could be proud of. After graduation, Akash joined a non-profit organization working on environmental conservation, focusing on protecting endangered species and restoring degraded ecosystems. His work was challenging, but he found immense fulfillment in contributing to a cause he believed in.

Akash's story highlights the power of living authentically, even when it means challenging the expectations of those closest to us. His journey illustrates the importance of aligning your actions with your values, of finding your purpose and pursuing it with unwavering conviction.

Then there's the story of Nisha, a young woman from a rural village in Uttar Pradesh. Her family was struggling financially, and Nisha, despite her dreams of higher education, was expected to contribute to the family income by marrying early and starting a family. But Nisha had other aspirations. She had always excelled academically, dreaming of becoming a teacher, of inspiring young minds.

She was determined to break the cycle of poverty and empower herself through education. She faced countless obstacles, from her family's resistance to societal norms that placed limitations on a young woman's ambitions.

Nisha refused to let her circumstances define her destiny. She persevered, seeking educational opportunities, studying late into the night, and overcoming every challenge with unwavering determination. Despite facing skepticism and disapproval, she completed her education, achieving her dream of becoming a teacher.

Nisha's story is a testament to the transformative power of education, of the courage to break free from societal limitations and pursue your own dreams. It is a powerful reminder that even in the most challenging circumstances, an authentic life, a life lived on your own terms, is within reach.

These are just a few stories, glimpses into the lives of individuals who dared to step out of the shadows and embrace their true selves. They remind us that authenticity is not a destination but a journey, a constant process of self-discovery and transformation. It is about understanding your values, embracing your uniqueness, and living in alignment with your true self.

The path towards authenticity is not always easy, but it is always worth it. It is a path filled with challenges, moments of doubt, and occasional setbacks. But it is also a path of immense growth, self-discovery, and fulfillment.

Remember Lesha, Akash, and Nisha. They are not exceptions but examples, reminding us that every individual has the potential to live an authentic life, a life filled with meaning, purpose, and joy.

The journey to live authentically begins with a simple but profound question: "Who am I?" Take the time to explore this question, to delve deep into your heart and soul, and discover the essence of who you truly are.

Embrace your uniqueness. Allow your individuality to shine, and let your authentic self-blossom.

Be brave. Challenge the expectations that hold you back. Let your values guide your choices, and live a life that aligns with your deepest desires.

Your journey to an authentic life is waiting. The courage to take that first step is all it takes.

<u>Overcoming Fear of Judgement:</u>

The fear of judgment is a powerful force that can hold us back from living our most authentic lives. It whispers doubts in our ears, urging us to conform, to shrink ourselves, to hide our true selves from the world. This fear is often rooted in a deep-seated need for acceptance, a yearning to be seen as "good" and "worthy" in the eyes of others. However, the pursuit of external validation can lead to a life that is inauthentic, a life where we are constantly performing, never truly comfortable in our own skin.

In India, where societal norms and expectations play a significant role, the fear of judgment can be particularly potent. We are raised with a sense of duty to uphold family honor, to adhere to traditional values, and to conform to the expectations of our community. These ingrained messages can create constant pressure to fit in, to avoid any actions that might bring shame upon ourselves or our families. As a result, many of us live with a constant sense of anxiety, afraid to express our true selves, afraid to pursue our passions, afraid to take risks that might deviate from the prescribed path.

But what does it truly mean to live authentically? It is not about becoming a rebel, rejecting all societal norms, or living in a constant state of defiance. Authenticity is about aligning our actions with our values, about embracing our strengths and weaknesses, and about living in accordance with our own truth. It is about honoring our individuality, our unique gifts and talents, and allowing them to shine, even if it means stepping outside of the box, even if it means facing judgment.

Overcoming the fear of judgment is a journey, not a destination. It requires courage, self-awareness, and a willingness to challenge our ingrained beliefs. Here are some steps we can take to begin this journey:

1. Recognize and Acknowledge the Fear:

The first step in overcoming any fear is acknowledging its presence. Take some time to reflect on your own experiences. What situations trigger feelings of anxiety or self-doubt? What voices in your head tell you to conform, to play it safe, to hide your true self? Once you have identified these triggers and patterns, you can begin to address them consciously.

2. Challenge Your Beliefs:

The fear of judgment often stems from deep-seated beliefs about ourselves and the world. These beliefs, often formed in childhood, can be deeply ingrained and resistant to change. Challenge these beliefs by asking yourself critical questions: Where do these beliefs come from? Are they based on evidence or on assumptions? What are the consequences of holding onto these beliefs? By questioning your beliefs, you can begin to break free from their limiting influence.

3. Embrace Imperfection:

The fear of judgment is often driven by the desire to be perfect, to be seen as flawless and worthy of admiration. However, this pursuit of perfection is a fool's errand. We are all flawed, and that is perfectly okay. Embrace your imperfections, your vulnerabilities, and your humanness. Allow yourself to make mistakes, to stumble, to fall. It is in these moments of imperfection that we truly discover our strength and resilience.

4. Surround Yourself with Supportive People:

The people we surround ourselves with have a profound impact on our sense of self-worth. If you are surrounded by people who constantly criticize, judge, or put you down, it will be much harder to overcome the fear of judgment. Seek out connections with people who are supportive, encouraging, and accepting of you for who you are. These relationships will provide the foundation you need to build confidence and to embrace your authentic self.

5. Practice Self-Compassion:

Being kind to yourself is essential in overcoming the fear of judgment. When you make a mistake, or when you feel self-doubt creeping in, treat yourself with the same kindness and compassion you would extend to a loved one. Talk to yourself in a soothing and encouraging voice. Remind yourself that you are human, that you are worthy of love and acceptance, and that you are on a journey of growth.

6. Step Outside of Your Comfort Zone:

The fear of judgment is often tied to the desire to stay within our comfort zones. But it is precisely in those uncomfortable, unfamiliar territories that we discover who we truly are. Challenge yourself to step outside of your comfort zone, to try new things, to take risks, to express yourself in ways you never have before. Each small step you take will build your confidence and resilience, paving the way for a more authentic and fulfilling life.

7. Remember Your Purpose:

Ultimately, the fear of judgment should not dictate our choices. We are all here with a unique purpose, a unique contribution to make to the world. When we focus on that purpose, when we align our actions with our values, the opinions of others fade into the background. The fear of judgment loses its power, and we are free to live our lives with integrity, passion, and authenticity.

Stories of Authentic Living:

There are countless stories of individuals who have overcome the fear of judgment and found fulfillment in living authentically. Let's explore a few:

The Story of Vani:

Vani was a young woman from a small village in Uttar Pradesh. She had always dreamt of becoming a doctor, but her family insisted that she should marry and become a homemaker. Despite the pressure, Vani refused to give up on her dream. She defied societal expectations, pursued her education, and eventually became a successful doctor. Her journey was not easy; she faced criticism, judgment, and even ostracism from her community. But she persevered, staying true to her values and her purpose. Vani's story is a powerful reminder that it is possible to overcome the fear of judgment and to live a life that is true to oneself.

The Story of Ajit:

Ajit was a young man from Mumbai who felt trapped in a career he hated. He worked as a software engineer, a job that he found unfulfilling and soul-crushing. He dreamed of becoming a musician, but he was afraid to pursue his passion because he feared the judgment of his family and friends. He worried that they would think he was irresponsible, that he was throwing away his future. But Ajit eventually realized that he couldn't live a life that was not his own. He took a leap of faith, quit his job, and enrolled in a music school. He faced challenges and doubts, but he never gave up on his dream. Ajit's story is a testament to the power of following our hearts, even when it means facing judgment.

The Story of Veena:

Veena was a young woman from Delhi who struggled with her sexuality. She was attracted to women, but she grew up in a society that did not accept homosexuality. She felt isolated and ashamed, afraid to reveal her true self for fear of rejection and condemnation. Veena lived a double life, hiding her true identity from her family and friends. But as she grew older, she realized that she could no longer live a lie. She came out to her loved ones, and while she faced challenges and hurt, she also found acceptance, support, and a sense of liberation. Veena's story is a powerful reminder that we must embrace our authentic selves, even if it means defying societal norms.

Overcoming the Fear of Judgment: A Lifelong Journey:

Living authentically is a lifelong journey, a constant process of self-discovery and self-acceptance. There will be times when we will falter, when we will succumb to the whispers of doubt and fear. But with each step we take, with each act of courage, we move closer to a life that is truly our own. By recognizing the fear of judgment, challenging our limiting beliefs, embracing imperfection, surrounding ourselves with supportive people, practicing self-compassion, stepping outside of our comfort zones, and remembering our purpose, we can begin to break free from the shackles of judgment and embrace the liberating power of authenticity.

Aligning Actions with Values:

The pursuit of authenticity is a journey of self-discovery, a constant exploration of who we truly are and how we align our actions with our deepest values. It's a journey that often leads us through difficult terrain, challenging us to confront our fears, shed societal expectations, and embrace the liberating power of being true to ourselves.

> Imagine a young woman named **Kiran**, growing up in a bustling city in India. She's always been a bright, ambitious student, excelling in academics. But the pressure to follow a traditional career path, a path that led to a stable job and a secure future, weighed heavily upon her. She felt an unspoken expectation to pursue a career in medicine or engineering, fields that promised a respectable life in the eyes of her family and community. Yet, her heart yearned for something different, something that ignited her passion and allowed her to express her creativity. She had a deep love for music, a talent that she had nurtured since childhood. But the idea of pursuing a career in music seemed almost ludicrous in her family's eyes. It was considered a frivolous pursuit, an unstable path that wouldn't provide the financial security and social status they valued.

Kiran felt trapped in this conflict. She knew that following her heart would mean defying societal norms and facing disapproval from her family. Yet, the thought of spending her life in a profession that didn't ignite her soul filled her with a sense of dread. The fear of judgment, the fear of disappointing her loved ones, held her captive. But within her, a quiet voice persisted, urging her to listen to her own desires, to believe in the power of her dreams.

Kiran found solace in the writings of a renowned author, a voice that resonated with her own inner struggle. The author spoke about the importance of aligning actions with values, about embracing the courage to live authentically. It was a simple concept, yet it held profound power. Kiran realized that living an authentic life meant being true to herself, regardless of the external pressures and expectations. It meant honoring her own values, even if they diverged from the conventional norms of her society.

She took a deep breath and made a decision. She would follow her passion for music. It wouldn't be an easy path, but she was determined to create a life that was aligned with her values. She started by taking small steps, enrolling in music classes, joining local bands, and sharing her music with friends and family. The journey was filled with challenges, moments of doubt, and criticism from those who didn't understand her choice. But Kiran persevered, fueled by her passion and the unwavering belief in her ability to create a meaningful life on her own terms.

Kiran's story is not unique. It's a story that resonates with many individuals across the globe, people who struggle to reconcile their own desires with the expectations of their families, communities, and societies. The journey towards authenticity often begins with a simple question: What are my core values? What principles guide my life? And how can I ensure that my actions reflect these values?

For some, the answer may be clear and straightforward. For others, it may require deep introspection, a process of self-discovery that can be both challenging and rewarding. We may find that our values are rooted in our cultural heritage, our upbringing, or our personal experiences. They may be shaped by our beliefs about what is right and wrong, what is important and meaningful.

Once we have a clear understanding of our values, the next step is to align our actions with them. This involves a conscious effort to make choices that reflect our deepest beliefs. It may mean challenging ourselves to step outside of our comfort zones, to break free from societal norms, or to confront our own fears.

Let's explore this concept through a framework, a roadmap to guide us on this journey of aligning actions with values:

1. **Identifying Core Values**: Begin by reflecting on what truly matters to you. What principles do you live by? What are your priorities in life? Consider values such as integrity, honesty, compassion, creativity, knowledge, growth, and purpose. These are just a few examples; the list will be unique to each individual.

2. **Analyzing Actions**: Once you have identified your core values, take a closer look at your daily actions. Do your actions align with these values? Are you living in accordance with your principles? Be honest with yourself as you analyze your daily routine, your choices, and your behaviors.

3. **Identifying Gaps**: You may discover that there are gaps between your values and your actions. For example, if one of your core values is integrity, but you find yourself engaging in dishonest behavior, you have identified a gap that needs to be addressed.

4. **Making Adjustments**: The next step is to make adjustments to your actions, to bring them into alignment with your values. This may involve making difficult choices, challenging yourself to step outside of your comfort zone, or seeking support from trusted individuals who can help you along the way.

5. **Constant Reflection**: Living authentically is not a one-time event. It's an ongoing process of reflection and adjustment. Take time to regularly evaluate your actions and ensure that they are aligned with your values. Life is a journey of constant growth and evolution, and our values may shift and evolve over time.

Living a life aligned with our values isn't always easy. It often requires courage, self-awareness, and a willingness to challenge the status quo. But the rewards are immense. We experience a sense of deep fulfillment, a sense of purpose and meaning in our lives. We become empowered to create a life that is true to our authentic selves.

Here are some practical tips for aligning your actions with your values:

Set Intentions: Start each day with a clear intention to live in alignment with your values. Consider what you want to achieve that day and how you can ensure your actions reflect your principles.

Make Conscious Choices: Be mindful of your choices, both big and small. Consider how your choices impact your values and whether they are consistent with your beliefs.

Practice Self-Reflection: Take time to reflect on your actions and behaviors. Ask yourself: "Am I living in accordance with my values?" "What adjustments can I make to bring my actions into alignment with my beliefs?"

Seek Support: Don't be afraid to seek support from trusted friends, family members, or mentors. Talk to people who share your values or who can offer guidance and encouragement.

Embrace Imperfection: Remember that we are all human and we will make mistakes. The journey towards authenticity is not about achieving perfection but about striving to live in alignment with our values as much as possible. Be kind to yourself, learn from your mistakes, and keep moving forward.

Aligning actions with values is a transformative journey. It's a journey that requires courage, self-awareness, and a commitment to living a life that is true to our authentic selves. It's a journey that can lead to a life filled with meaning, purpose, and deep fulfillment.

Creating a Life of Integrity:

The quest for authenticity is a lifelong journey. It's about aligning our actions with our values, living in accordance with our true selves, and creating a life that reflects our deepest desires. To live authentically is to embrace our imperfections, acknowledge our strengths, and allow our unique essence to shine through.

Creating a life of integrity involves a conscious effort to build a foundation of truthfulness, consistency, and moral soundness. It's about living in alignment with our values, making choices that reflect our beliefs, and maintaining a strong sense of self-respect.

This process begins with self-awareness. We need to understand our values, our strengths, and our weaknesses. What are the principles that guide our actions? What are the things we stand for? What kind of person do we want to be? When we have a clear understanding of our core values, we can begin to make choices that align with them.

It's also important to be honest with ourselves about our weaknesses. We all have flaws and imperfections. But by acknowledging them, we can begin to work towards improving ourselves. We can cultivate self-discipline, learn from our mistakes, and strive to be better versions of ourselves.

Integrity isn't just about personal values; it's also about our relationships with others. It's about being honest and transparent in our interactions, keeping our promises, and treating others with respect, even when it's difficult.

Here are some practical tips for building a life of integrity:

Be truthful: Honesty is the foundation of integrity. Be truthful with yourself and others, even when it's uncomfortable.

Keep your promises: When you make a promise, do your best to keep it. This builds trust and strengthens your relationships.

Take responsibility for your actions: Don't blame others for your mistakes. Take responsibility for your actions, learn from them, and strive to do better in the future.

Be consistent: Integrity involves being consistent in our actions and behaviors. Our words and deeds should reflect the same values.

Be respectful: Treat others with respect, even when you disagree with them. Listen to their perspectives, acknowledge their feelings, and strive to understand their viewpoints.

Be compassionate: Compassion involves understanding and sharing the feelings of others. It's about extending empathy and kindness to those around us.

Be forgiving: Forgiveness is essential for personal growth and healthy relationships. It's about letting go of resentment and bitterness and moving forward with a clean slate.

Building a life of integrity is an ongoing process, not a destination. It requires ongoing self-reflection, conscious effort, and a commitment to living in alignment with our values. It may involve making difficult choices and facing challenges, but the rewards are immeasurable.

Living authentically is a journey of self-discovery, growth, and fulfillment. It's about being true to ourselves, embracing our imperfections, and living in accordance with our values. When we live with integrity, we create a life that is not only personally fulfilling but also contributes positively to the world around us.

Take a moment to reflect on your own life. Are your actions aligned with your values? Are you living authentically? Are you making choices that reflect the kind of person you want to be? If not, take steps to create a life of integrity, a life that is truly your own.

Story of Asha:

Asha, a young woman from a small village in Uttar Pradesh, faced a common dilemma in her life – the pressure to conform to societal expectations. From a young age, she had been taught that her primary role was to be a dutiful daughter, a devoted wife, and a nurturing mother. She was expected to prioritize her family's needs above her own and to accept a life of quiet domesticity.

Asha, however, harbored a deep passion for art. She loved to paint, to express her emotions through vibrant colors and creative compositions. However, she knew that her family would disapprove. They believed art to be frivolous, impractical, and a distraction from her "real" responsibilities.

Asha found herself living a life of silent discontent. She felt a sense of unease within her, a yearning for something more, a yearning to express her true self.

One day, a visiting art teacher noticed Asha's talent and encouraged her to pursue her passion. The teacher's words resonated with Asha. She realized that she couldn't keep her true self hidden any longer.

Asha's decision to follow her passion was not easy. She faced resistance from her family, who believed she was making a foolish choice. She was told that she would regret it, that she would be judged, that she would never succeed.

Asha, however, was determined. She knew that to live a life of integrity, she had to follow her heart. She began to paint in secret, taking classes in the evenings, and attending art exhibitions in the city. Slowly, her confidence grew, and her talent blossomed.

Despite facing obstacles, Asha never gave up. She continued to practice her art, honing her skills, and exhibiting her work whenever possible. Her passion and her dedication eventually earned her recognition. She received awards for her artwork, her work was featured in local galleries, and she even had an opportunity to exhibit her work in the city.

Asha's success, however, was not just about the recognition she received. It was about the fulfillment she found in expressing her true self. She had created a life that was in alignment with her values. She had overcome the fear of judgment and the pressure to conform.

Asha's story is a powerful reminder that living authentically is not always easy. It often requires courage, determination, and a willingness to challenge societal norms. But by embracing our true selves and creating lives that reflect our values, we can find a sense of purpose, fulfillment, and inner peace.

Story of Shivam:

Shivam, a successful businessman, had built a life that most would envy. He had a beautiful wife, two lovely children, a luxurious home, and a thriving business. He had achieved financial success beyond his wildest dreams, and he had everything he thought he ever wanted.

However, Shivam felt a deep sense of emptiness inside. He had achieved everything he had set out to do, but he didn't feel truly happy. He realized that he had spent so much time chasing external success that he had neglected his personal growth and his inner self.

Shivam began to question the values that had guided his life. He realized that his focus on material possessions and financial success had left him feeling unfulfilled. He was living a life that was not in alignment with his true self.

Shivam decided to make a change. He began to prioritize his personal growth, spending time on his hobbies, exploring his passions, and nurturing his relationships. He also started to practice mindfulness and meditation to connect with his inner self.

Shivam 's journey of self-discovery led him to a new understanding of what true success meant. He learned that true success was not just about material possessions and financial achievements but also about living a life of purpose, authenticity, and integrity.

Shivam's story is a reminder that material possessions and external achievements don't guarantee happiness. True fulfillment comes from living a life that is in alignment with our values, embracing our true selves, and making a positive impact on the world around us.

The Path to Integrity:

Creating a life of integrity is an ongoing journey, a path that we must continuously navigate. It's not about being perfect; it's about being honest with ourselves, owning our flaws, and striving to be better versions of ourselves each day.

It involves making conscious choices, taking responsibility for our actions, and building relationships based on trust and respect. It requires courage to speak our truth, to challenge our limiting beliefs, and to break free from societal pressures.

As we embark on this journey, we may stumble, we may make mistakes. But we must not be afraid to learn from our experiences and to grow from them.

Ultimately, the path to integrity is a path to fulfillment, a path to a life that is truly our own. It's a path worth taking, and it's a path that can lead to a life of purpose, authenticity, and profound happiness.

10

LIVING BEYOND THE BRACKETS

The End of Self-Imposed Limits:

The air hangs heavy with the weight of expectations, the whispers of what we *should* be, and the echoes of societal norms that we've internalized as our own truths. But what if those truths, those invisible boundaries we've constructed around ourselves, are merely a reflection of fear? What if the fear of stepping outside the comfort zone, of defying expectations, and of challenging our own beliefs is the very thing that keeps us trapped within a self-imposed prison?

> Imagine a young woman named **Ganga**, raised in a small village in Maharashtra. Her world was painted in shades of tradition, where a woman's role was defined by domesticity and societal expectations. But Priya felt a pull towards something more, a yearning for a life beyond the familiar boundaries. The seeds of discontent were sown in her heart, a quiet rebellion against the preordained script of her life.

Ganga's story is a familiar one, resonating with countless individuals who grapple with the weight of expectations, the pressure to conform, and the fear of defying the norms. But Ganga's journey is unique, as she decided to confront the invisible bars of her own self-imposed limitations. It wasn't an easy decision; it was a choice made with trembling hands and a heart pounding with both excitement and trepidation.

Ganga decided to enroll in an art school in Mumbai, defying the expectations of her family and community. The decision was met with resistance, with whispers of disapproval, and with fear that she was jeopardizing her future. Yet, Ganga refused to let those whispers drown out the powerful voice within her.

The journey was fraught with challenges, the pressure to conform was relentless, and the fear of failure lurked in the shadows. But Ganga persevered, fueled by an unyielding belief in her own abilities and an unwavering determination to break free from the shackles of self-imposed limitations.

Ganga's story is a testament to the resilience of the human spirit, the strength found in embracing change, and the courage to live authentically. It is a story that echoes the universal desire for self-expression, for personal fulfillment, and for a life that reflects our true selves.

But Ganga's journey is not merely a tale of individual triumph, it's a reflection of the collective struggle we all face in navigating the complexities of life, in navigating the expectations that bind us, and in finding the courage to break free from the invisible cages we construct around ourselves.

Our self-imposed limitations are often a product of our fears, the fears of judgment, of failure, and of disappointing those we love. We create mental boundaries, invisible walls that keep us safe, yet simultaneously restrict our potential. We fear the unknown, the uncomfortable, and the possibility of venturing outside our comfort zones.

This fear can manifest in countless ways: the fear of pursuing a dream career, the fear of leaving a secure job, the fear of expressing ourselves authentically, the fear of challenging societal norms, the fear of confronting our own beliefs, the fear of being judged.

These fears become the invisible shackles that bind us, chains forged from our own anxieties and doubts. They whisper lies in our ears, telling us that we are not capable, that we are not enough, that we should stay within the confines of what we know.

But the truth is, we are capable of so much more. We are capable of exceeding our own expectations, of challenging our own beliefs, of breaking free from the self-imposed limits that have held us captive for so long.

The journey of breaking free is not always easy, it can be fraught with challenges and setbacks. But it is a journey worth taking, a journey that leads to a more fulfilling and authentic life.

The first step in this journey is recognizing the existence of these invisible boundaries. We need to become aware of the fears that hold us back, the beliefs that limit us, and the expectations that weigh us down. This awareness is crucial, it allows us to confront our fears and begin the process of dismantling the walls we have erected around ourselves.

Once we become aware of these limitations, we can begin to challenge them. We can question our beliefs, explore new perspectives, and embrace the unknown. We can step out of our comfort zones, embrace calculated risks, and pursue our passions, regardless of the potential for judgment or failure.

Breaking free is not a one-time event, it is an ongoing process of self-discovery, of growth, and of transformation. It is a journey that requires courage, resilience, and an unwavering belief in our own abilities.

As we journey beyond our self-imposed limits, we begin to discover the boundless possibilities that life offers. We realize that the comfort zone, while providing a sense of safety, can also be a breeding ground for stagnation and missed opportunities. Stepping outside of our comfort zones allows us to embrace new experiences, to learn and grow, and to discover new aspects of ourselves.

This journey is not about abandoning our values or compromising our beliefs. It is about challenging our assumptions, broadening our perspectives, and becoming more open to the possibilities that lie beyond the confines of our own limited vision. It is about embracing the beauty of diversity, the power of empathy, and the importance of living authentically.

The journey beyond the brackets is a journey of self-discovery, a journey of growth, a journey of transformation. It is a journey that leads to a more fulfilling and authentic life, a life that is lived on our own terms.

We are not meant to be confined by the limitations we impose upon ourselves. We are meant to explore, to grow, to evolve, and to embrace the boundless possibilities that life offers. The journey beyond the brackets is a journey of liberation, a journey of self-discovery, a journey of becoming the best version of ourselves. It is a journey that starts with the courage to challenge our assumptions, to break free from the confines of our comfort zones, and to embrace the infinite possibilities that lie beyond the invisible walls we have built around ourselves.

It's a journey that starts with a single step, a step outside the familiar, a step towards the unknown, a step towards a life that reflects our true selves.

<u>Inspirational Stories of Transformation:</u>

The air crackled with anticipation as **Shree**, a seasoned doctor, finally took the plunge. After years of diligently serving at the local hospital, she had decided to leave the familiar comfort of her job and dedicate herself to setting up a free clinic in a remote village. It was a decision that had been brewing in her heart for years, fueled by a quiet passion for helping those most in need.

Shree's colleagues had tried to dissuade her, warning her of the challenges and sacrifices she would face. The village, situated in a rugged mountainous region, lacked basic amenities, and the local population had limited access to healthcare. But Shree was undeterred. The weight of societal expectations, the allure of a stable career, and the fear of the unknown couldn't hold her back. She had chosen to live beyond the brackets of her comfort zone, driven by an internal compass that pointed towards a life of purpose and service.

As she settled into the village, Shree's initial trepidation gave way to an inspiring sense of purpose. The villagers, initially hesitant, gradually warmed up to her, drawn to her genuine care and dedication. The clinic, initially a humble space, became a lifeline for the community, providing much-needed healthcare, but also a platform for social connection and empowerment. Shree's journey wasn't without its struggles. The lack of resources, the grueling work schedule, and the constant challenges of navigating a new environment tested her resilience. Yet, she persevered, her spirit fueled by the gratitude in the eyes of the people she served.

In the quiet of her humble quarters, Shree would often reflect on her journey. It was a journey of self-discovery, a testament to the power of challenging self-imposed limitations. The societal norms that had once defined her path had gradually dissolved, replaced by a deep sense of purpose and fulfillment. Shree's story wasn't just about leaving a job; it was about leaving behind the shackles of fear and embracing the boundless possibilities that lay beyond the familiar.

Across the country, in the bustling metropolis of Mumbai, a young man named **Rajan** was struggling to find his place in the world. Raised in a family of entrepreneurs, he had been expected to follow in their footsteps, but his heart lay elsewhere. The allure of a corporate career, the promise of financial stability, and the pressure to live up to family expectations had weighed heavily on him.

Rajan had always felt drawn to the arts, particularly music. He yearned to express himself through melody and rhythm, but the fear of judgment, the doubts about his talent, and the societal stigma associated with pursuing an unconventional path kept him trapped in a box of his own making. As he navigated the corporate world, Rajan felt a growing dissonance within him. His job, despite the material success it brought, felt hollow, lacking the spark that his soul craved.

One evening, as he was drowning his anxieties in a local pub, he stumbled upon a small band playing traditional Indian music. The raw energy, the soulful melodies, and the palpable joy on the faces of the musicians struck a chord within him. That night, Rajan made a decision. He decided to shed the expectations that had been placed upon him and follow his heart's calling.

With trepidation but a growing sense of purpose, Rajan quit his corporate job and enrolled in a music school. The transition wasn't easy. His family was disappointed, his friends skeptical, and his own doubts lingered. But Rajan persevered. He immersed himself in the world of music, absorbing knowledge, honing his skills, and embracing the joy of creative expression.

Years later, Rajan, known as " Rajan the Raga," became a celebrated musician, his soulful melodies touching the hearts of audiences across the country. He had defied the expectations, embraced his passion, and found fulfillment in living a life true to himself. Rajan's story was a testament to the power of breaking free from societal norms, trusting one's intuition, and embracing the adventure of following one's own path.

In a small town in Kerala, a young woman named **Revathi** was battling her own internal struggles. Brought up in a traditional household, Revathi had been taught that a woman's place was in the home, nurturing her family and fulfilling the role of a wife and mother. Her education, her ambition, and her desire for a career outside the domestic sphere had been gently but firmly discouraged.

Revathi, a bright and ambitious young woman, felt a growing sense of frustration and discontent. She yearned to break free from the confines of societal expectations, to pursue her dreams, and to create a life of her own making. The weight of tradition, the fear of judgment, and the internalized beliefs that had shaped her upbringing held her captive.

One day, Revathi stumbled upon an online article about a woman who had started her own small business, defying societal norms and creating a successful career for herself. The story ignited a spark within Revathi, a sense of possibility and a realization that her own dreams were not unattainable.

With a newfound determination, Revathi decided to take the plunge. She enrolled in a business management course, learning about entrepreneurship and the challenges and rewards of starting a company. She poured her heart and soul into her studies, finding strength in her own ambition and a growing sense of self-belief.

After months of preparation, Revathi launched her own small bakery, named "Revathi's Delights." The bakery, with its tempting aroma of fresh bread and pastries, quickly became a local favorite, its success a testament to Revathi's talent and entrepreneurial spirit. Revathi's journey wasn't just about starting a business; it was about breaking free from limiting beliefs, challenging societal norms, and embracing the power of her own aspirations.

These stories of transformation, of individuals breaking free from self-imposed limitations and societal expectations, were not isolated incidents. Across India, countless individuals were embarking on their own journeys of self-discovery and personal growth, rewriting their narratives and creating lives of purpose and fulfillment. They were living beyond the brackets of their comfort zones, challenging the status quo, and embracing the infinite possibilities that life offered.

As you embark on your own journey, remember Shree's unwavering dedication, Rajan's courage to follow his heart, and Revathi's determination to break free from societal norms. Their stories serve as a powerful reminder that the power to shape your own destiny lies within you. You have the strength to challenge your own limitations, to embrace change, and to create a life that is truly authentic and fulfilling. The world is waiting to witness the brilliance you hold within.

<u>Embracing Infinite Possibilities:</u>

The world is a vast and ever-expanding tapestry of experiences, possibilities, and opportunities waiting to be explored. We are each a unique thread within this intricate design, woven into a story that is ours alone to create. However, too often, we limit ourselves, constructing invisible brackets around our lives that confine us to a narrow view of what is possible. We become accustomed to the familiar, settling for the comfort of routines and expectations, inadvertently shutting out the boundless potential that lies beyond.

> Imagine a young woman named **Lata**, growing up in a small village in rural India. Her life was defined by the familiar rhythms of village life - tending to the fields, helping her mother with chores, and attending the local school. She dreamt of becoming a doctor, her heart yearning for the knowledge and skills to heal others. Yet, the voices of her family, her community, and the ingrained societal expectations whispered a different narrative. They saw her as destined to become a wife, a homemaker, fulfilling the traditional roles expected of women. The weight of these expectations, like invisible chains, bound her to a predetermined path.

The comfort of familiarity and the fear of defying societal norms kept her trapped within a self-imposed bracket. She felt the pull of her dreams, the yearning to break free, yet the societal pressure held her back. It wasn't until she met a visiting doctor, a woman who had defied expectations and achieved her dreams, that Lata began to see the possibilities beyond the limitations she had accepted. The doctor's story sparked a fire within Lata, igniting a newfound belief in her own capabilities.

Lata 's story is a reflection of many others. It speaks to the universal struggle of navigating societal pressures and self-imposed boundaries. But it also highlights the liberating power of breaking free from those limitations, of embracing the infinite possibilities that life offers. It's about daring to step beyond the familiar, to challenge the constraints of tradition, and to embrace the adventure of living a life that is authentically ours.

The journey beyond the brackets requires courage, a willingness to question the norms we've been taught, and a belief in our own potential. It's about recognizing that our lives are not bound by the expectations of others, but by the dreams we hold within our hearts. It's about embracing the unknown, stepping into the realm of infinite possibilities with open arms and a curious mind.

This journey isn't about discarding everything we've been taught or rejecting the values that have shaped us. It's about finding our own unique path, honoring our roots while allowing ourselves to grow and evolve. It's about embracing the beauty of diversity, recognizing the value of different perspectives, and understanding that the richness of life lies in its infinite possibilities.

It's about embracing the challenges and setbacks as learning experiences, seeing them as opportunities for growth and redirection. It's about recognizing our own strengths and weaknesses, using our unique talents to contribute to the world in meaningful ways. It's about choosing to live a life of purpose, one that is aligned with our values and aspirations, a life that leaves a positive mark on the world.

The world is waiting for us to break free from our self-imposed limitations, to unleash the power of our dreams and aspirations. It's waiting for us to live a life beyond the brackets, to embrace the infinite possibilities that lie before us.

> Let's consider another example, that of **Kamal**, a young man who grew up in a middle-class family in Mumbai. His parents, like countless others, harbored dreams of a secure future for their son. They envisioned him becoming a doctor or an engineer, professions they believed would guarantee a comfortable life. Kamal, however, harbored a different dream. He was passionate about art, drawn to the expressive power of colors and forms. He spent countless hours sketching, painting, and immersing himself in the world of creativity.

However, the pressure to fulfill his parents' expectations, to live up to the societal norms that valued academic achievement above all else, kept Kamal trapped within a self-imposed bracket. He felt a constant pull between his own aspirations and the expectations that surrounded him. He feared disappointing his family, yet he couldn't ignore the yearning within his soul.

This internal conflict led Kamal to a crossroads. He could follow the path laid out for him, securing a stable future but sacrificing his passion. Or he could choose to embrace his true self, pursue his artistic dreams, and risk the disapproval of his family and the societal expectations he had internalized. It was a difficult decision, a choice that would shape the course of his life.

Kamal's story, like Lata's, speaks to the common struggle of navigating the expectations of others while pursuing our own unique passions. It showcases the courage it takes to break free from self-imposed limitations and embrace the unknown. It's about recognizing that our lives are not confined to predefined paths, but are open to infinite possibilities.

As Kamal wrestled with his decision, he discovered that he wasn't alone. He found solace in the stories of others who had dared to defy expectations, who had chosen to live life on their own terms. He learned that it was possible to find fulfillment and success beyond the conventional boundaries.

Inspired by their stories, Kamal took a leap of faith. He chose to embrace his artistic passion, seeking out opportunities to learn and grow. He enrolled in an art school, immersing himself in the world of creativity. While he faced challenges and moments of doubt, he never lost sight of his dreams. He learned to navigate the disapproval of his family, to create his own path, and to define success on his own terms.

Kamal's journey highlights the transformative power of breaking free from self-imposed limitations. It reminds us that our lives are not meant to be lived within the confines of expectations, but to be embraced in all their vibrant complexity.

The journeys of Lata and Kamal, though different, offer a glimpse into the shared human experience of navigating societal pressures and self-imposed limitations. Their stories are a testament to the power of breaking free from those constraints, of embracing the unknown, and of living a life that is authentically ours.

The path beyond the brackets may not always be easy. There will be challenges, setbacks, and moments of doubt. However, it's in those moments that we discover our inner strength, our resilience, and our ability to create a life that is truly fulfilling.

As we move forward, let us remember that we are not limited by the expectations of others or by the boundaries we create for ourselves. We have the power to define our own paths, to break free from the constraints of societal norms, and to embrace the infinite possibilities that life offers. Let us be bold, curious, and compassionate, living a life that is authentic, purposeful, and aligned with our deepest dreams.

<u>Building a Vision for the Future:</u>

The concept of living beyond the brackets is not just about dismantling limitations imposed by society, but also about breaking free from the self-imposed boundaries we construct around ourselves. It's about recognizing the vast potential within and allowing it to unfold. It's about letting go of the fear of uncertainty and embracing the infinite possibilities that life offers.

Imagine a canvas, pristine and white, ready to be painted with the colors of your dreams. Your vision for the future is like that canvas – a blank slate where you can sketch the life you desire, the aspirations you wish to achieve, and the impact you want to make on the world.

But before we begin to paint, we must first understand what we want to create. This involves a deep introspection, a journey into the depths of your heart and soul to uncover the desires that have been waiting to be expressed.

1. The Power of Vision:

A vision for the future is not merely a wish list, it's a roadmap. It's a clear and compelling picture of what you want your life to look like, a destination you strive to reach. It provides direction, motivation, and a sense of purpose, guiding you through the inevitable twists and turns of life.

> **Think Beyond the Immediate:** The first step is to liberate yourself from the constraints of the present moment. Step back from the daily grind and allow your mind to wander into the realm of possibilities. Imagine yourself five years from now, ten years from now, even twenty years from now. What does your life look like?

What are you doing? Where are you? Who are you with?

Visualize the Details: Don't limit yourself to vague aspirations. Be specific. What kind of home do you live in? What kind of work brings you joy? What kind of relationships nourish your soul? Allow your imagination to paint vivid details, filling in the picture with as much richness and clarity as possible.

Embrace Your Authentic Self: Your vision must be aligned with your true self, your core values, and your passions. It's not about fulfilling someone else's expectations or conforming to societal norms. It's about living a life that resonates with your deepest desires and brings you a sense of fulfillment.

2. The Art of Exploration:

Your vision for the future isn't set in stone. It's a living document that evolves and grows with you. You can't simply create a blueprint and expect it to remain unchanged. It's an ongoing process of exploration, discovery, and refinement.

Explore Your Interests: What brings you joy? What are you passionate about? What talents do you possess? What are you curious to learn more about? Dig deep within yourself and explore the diverse aspects of your being. Let your interests guide your vision, shaping it into a path that leads you towards a life you truly love.

Seek Inspiration: Inspiration is everywhere. Look to nature, art, music, literature, and the lives of people who have lived fulfilling lives. Read biographies, watch documentaries, listen to inspiring talks. Let their stories ignite your own dreams and inspire you to create a vision that reflects your unique potential.

Embrace the Unknown: Life is full of surprises, and that's part of its beauty. Don't be afraid to embrace the unknown. Let your vision be a framework for your journey, not a rigid plan. Be open to new opportunities, embrace change, and allow your vision to evolve as you navigate the unpredictable terrain of life.

3. The Power of Action:

A vision without action is a mere dream. It's the bridge between the present and the future. It's the force that propels you forward, turning your aspirations into reality.

Set Clear Goals: Once you have a vision for the future, break it down into smaller, actionable goals. Define specific steps you can take to achieve your aspirations. Set deadlines and track your progress, keeping your vision alive and motivating you to move forward.

Embrace the Process: The journey towards achieving your vision is often arduous and filled with challenges. Embrace the process, learn from your setbacks, and celebrate your successes. It's not about reaching the destination but about the growth and transformation that happens along the way.

Seek Support: Surround yourself with people who believe in you and your vision. Seek mentorship, guidance, and support from friends, family, and community members. Sharing your vision with others can help you stay motivated and accountable, and it can also lead to unexpected opportunities and connections.

4. Building a Life of Purpose:

A vision for the future isn't just about personal fulfillment; it's about creating a life of purpose. It's about aligning your aspirations with something bigger than yourself, contributing to the world in a meaningful way.

Identify Your Values: What are the values that guide your life? What do you believe in? What kind of impact do you want to make on the world? Aligning your vision with your core values ensures that you are living a life that is true to your beliefs and contributes to something you deeply care about.

Find Your Purpose: Purpose is not a destination, it's a journey. It's about discovering what you're meant to do, the unique contribution you can make to the world. It's about finding your passion, your calling, and aligning your vision with that purpose.

Embrace Service: Living a life of purpose is not just about achieving your own goals. It's about connecting with something bigger than yourself, contributing to the well-being of others. Seek opportunities to serve your community, support causes you believe in, and make a positive impact on the lives of others.

Creating a Vision for the Future: A Practical Guide:

Now that we've explored the essence of creating a vision for the future, let's delve into some practical steps you can take to bring your vision to life.

1. Reflect and Journal:

Dedicate time each day to quiet reflection. Sit in a peaceful space, close your eyes, and allow your mind to wander. Reflect on your values, your passions, your dreams, and your fears.

Keep a journal to record your thoughts and insights. Write about your aspirations, your fears, your successes, and your setbacks. Journaling allows you to process your emotions, clarify your thoughts, and gain a deeper understanding of yourself.

2. Dream Big and Be Specific:

Don't limit yourself to small, achievable goals. Dream big and imagine a future that fills you with excitement and inspiration.

As you visualize your future, be specific. What will your daily life look like? What kind of relationships will you have? What kind of work will you be doing? What will your home look like? The more specific you are, the clearer your vision will be.

3. Create a Vision Board:

Gather images, quotes, and objects that represent your vision. Create a physical or digital collage that symbolizes your aspirations and the life you want to create.

Place your vision board in a prominent location where you can see it every day. It serves as a constant reminder of your dreams and keeps you motivated to take action.

4. Set Smart Goals:

Once you have a clear vision, break it down into smaller, more manageable goals. Each goal should be Specific, Measurable, Achievable, Relevant, and Time-bound (SMART).

For example, if your vision is to start your own business, you might set a SMART goal to "Develop a business plan within three months and launch my online store by the end of the year."

5. Take Action and Track Progress:

Don't let your vision become a distant dream. Take action, even small steps, to move towards your goals.

Keep track of your progress. Celebrate your accomplishments, acknowledge your setbacks, and adjust your plan as needed.

Remember, creating a vision for the future is an ongoing process. It's a journey of discovery, growth, and transformation. Embrace the uncertainty, learn from your experiences, and never stop believing in your potential to create a life that is both fulfilling and meaningful.

Remember, the journey beyond the brackets is a personal one. It's about finding your voice, embracing your authenticity, and creating a life that resonates with your soul. It's a life where limitations are seen as opportunities, where comfort zones are transcended, and where the possibilities are infinite.

This is the essence of living beyond the brackets – a life of purpose, passion, and boundless potential. It's a life that is truly your own, a life that you have designed and created, a life that reflects the best version of yourself.

<u>Continuing the Legacy of Growth:</u>

The stories we've explored throughout this journey – tales of individuals who dared to break free from the shackles of their own limitations – are not merely narratives of personal transformation but beacons of inspiration. They serve as a testament to the boundless possibilities that lie within each one of us, waiting to be unleashed. Each individual's journey is a testament to the human spirit's capacity for resilience, growth, and change. They are living embodiments of the transformative power that comes with embracing change, seeking new perspectives, and stepping boldly into the unknown.

It's crucial to understand that the journey beyond the brackets isn't a destination, but a continuous exploration. It's an ongoing process of self-discovery, of constantly challenging our beliefs and pushing our boundaries. The individuals who have inspired us in this book have not reached a static endpoint; they are continuously evolving, adapting, and shaping their lives according to their own unique visions.

The act of living beyond the brackets isn't confined to the individual; it has the potential to create a ripple effect, impacting the lives of those around us. When we choose to live authentically and embrace our unique potential, we inspire others to do the same. We become catalysts for change, encouraging others to question the familiar, to challenge their own limitations, and to embark on their own journeys of personal growth.

Think of a young woman in a small village in rural India who, inspired by the stories of women entrepreneurs in this book, decides to break free from the traditional expectations placed upon her. She takes a leap of faith, starting her own small business, defying societal norms and paving the way for other women in her community to pursue their own dreams. Her story becomes a beacon of hope, igniting a spark of courage in others, prompting them to see the possibilities that lie beyond their perceived limitations.

Or imagine a young man, struggling with societal pressures to conform to a specific career path, finds inspiration in the stories of those who dared to follow their passions. He takes a chance, pursuing a career in a field he truly loves, defying societal expectations and proving to himself that he can achieve happiness and fulfillment by living on his own terms. His story becomes a testament to the power of self-belief and the importance of following one's own compass, encouraging others to embrace their passions and to carve their own paths in life.

These stories, woven into the fabric of our society, serve as a powerful reminder that the journey beyond the brackets is not just an individual pursuit; it is a collective endeavor. When we choose to break free from our limitations and live authentically, we contribute to a world that is more open, more inclusive, and more supportive of individual growth and fulfillment.

The legacy of growth we leave behind is not measured by our material possessions or social status; it is measured by the impact we have on others, by the lives we inspire and the changes we catalyze. It is in the ripple effect of our actions, the courage we ignite in others, and the paths we illuminate for those who seek to break free from their own limitations.

This journey is not about achieving a perfect state of being but about embracing the imperfections, the challenges, and the constant evolution of life. It is about recognizing the immense potential that lies within each one of us, and using that potential to create a more fulfilling and meaningful life, not just for ourselves, but for those around us. It's about embracing the power of our collective stories, recognizing that each individual's journey of transformation has the potential to inspire and uplift the world around them.

The world needs more stories of courage, resilience, and self-discovery. It needs stories of individuals who dared to live beyond the brackets, who defied expectations and transformed their lives. It needs stories of individuals who chose to see the world beyond their own perceived limitations, who embraced diversity, cultivated empathy, and lived with purpose.

As you continue your own journey, remember the stories shared within these pages. Let them inspire you to embrace the unknown, to challenge your own beliefs, and to break free from the confines of your self-imposed limitations. Share your own stories of growth and transformation, allowing your journey to inspire others to embark on their own paths of self-discovery.

The world needs your story, your unique perspective, your journey beyond the brackets. Let your light shine brightly, illuminating the path for others to follow. And in doing so, we collectively contribute to a world where everyone has the freedom to live a life that is authentic, fulfilling, and true to their own essence.

ACKNOWLEDGEMENT

The journey to writing this book has been enriched by the invaluable support of many individuals. I extend my heartfelt gratitude to:

My husband, whose unwavering encouragement and understanding has been a constant source of inspiration while he heavily contributed to refining my writing and created relative contexts to the stories.

The countless individuals who shared their personal stories with me, allowing me to weave their experiences into the tapestry of this narrative. Your courage and vulnerability are truly inspiring.

The insightful mentors who have shaped my understanding of human psychology and societal dynamics, guiding me toward a deeper appreciation of the complexities we all face.

This book is dedicated to everyone who seeks to break free from the limitations they impose on themselves, to those who dare to challenge societal norms, and to those who strive for a life filled with meaning and purpose.

GLOSSARY

This glossary defines key terms used throughout the book, providing a shared understanding of concepts related to personal growth, societal dynamics, and cultural norms.

Comfort Zone: A metaphorical area of familiar thoughts, behaviors, and experiences that offers a sense of safety and predictability but can also limit personal growth.

Expectations: Beliefs and assumptions about oneself, others, and the world, often influenced by societal norms, family traditions, and personal experiences.

Belief System: A set of deeply held convictions and assumptions that shape perceptions and actions.

Limiting Beliefs: Beliefs that restrict personal growth and potential, often stemming from fear, prejudice, or cultural conditioning.

Empathy: The ability to understand and share the feelings of others, fostering connection and compassion.

Authenticity: The state of being true to oneself, embracing one's values, beliefs, and experiences without compromising integrity.

Self-Discovery: The process of exploring and understanding oneself, including one's strengths, weaknesses, values, and aspirations.

232

REFERENCES

The book draws upon various sources to provide a comprehensive understanding of the themes explored. These references include:

Academic research and literature on human psychology, sociology, cultural studies, and self-help.

Personal accounts and stories shared by individuals who have embarked on their own journeys of growth and transformation.

Inspiring examples of social change and empowerment from diverse communities across India.

AUTHOR BIOGRAPHY

Anki Jain is an Indian writer seasoned with insightful observations on societal dynamics and human psychology. With a background and a passion for storytelling, she weaves relatable narratives that resonate with Indian readers, exploring themes of cultural norms, personal growth, and the pursuit of a fulfilling life.

Her husband, co-author & editor, pen named **KOKO**, is a dedicated advocate for social change and believes in the power of individual transformation to create a more just and compassionate world. He has authored several articles exploring various aspects of human experience, including self-help, social commentary, and cultural analysis.

Their writing is characterized by a conversational and introspective tone, inviting readers to engage with their own inner journeys and to challenge the limitations they impose on themselves. Both of them are committed to fostering critical thinking, promoting empathy, and empowering individuals to live authentically and meaningfully.

Reach out to Authors: foranki@gmail.com | kokoforkp@gmail.com

BOOKS BY AUTHOR

SERIES

Unfortunately, how we Live

[LIFE] : living in the brackets

>PAST< : living in the yesters

"SELF" : living in the egotism

}LONE{ : living in the solitude

INDIVIDUAL TITLES

IKIGAI : finding your reason for being